D0637351

PRO-LIFE
CHRISTIANS

*"Before I formed thee in the bowels of
thy mother, I knew thee."* —Jeremias 1:5

Crossroads College
G.H. Cachiaras Memorial Library
920 Mayowood Road SW, Rochester MN 5590(
507-535-3331

Minnesota Bible College Library
920 Mayowood Rd SW
Rochester, MN 55902

PRO-LIFE CHRISTIANS

HEROES FOR THE PRE-BORN

By

Joe Gulotta

*"Can a woman forget her infant, so as
not to have pity on the son of her womb?
and if she should forget, yet will not I forget thee."* —Isaias 49:15

TAN BOOKS AND PUBLISHERS, INC.
Rockford, Illinois 61105

Copyright © 1992 by TAN Books and Publishers, Inc.

All rights reserved. No part of this book may be reproduced or transmitted in any form or by any means, electronic or mechanical, including photocopying, recording, or by any information storage or retrieval system, without permission in writing from the publisher.

ISBN: 0-89555-460-7

Library of Congress Catalog Card No.: 92-60212

Cover photos from left to right: Shari Richard, Dr. James Dobson, Mary Cunningham Agee.

Printed and bound in the United States of America.

TAN BOOKS AND PUBLISHERS, INC.
P.O. Box 424
Rockford, Illinois 61105
1992

Dedication

This book is dedicated
To the Helen Doyles of the Pro-Life movement.

Acknowledgments

I would like to render special thanks to my parents, to Thomas A. Nelson, the Publisher of this book, to Anthony and Anita Mioni and to Bruce and Jane Browning. Other special acknowledgments go to Lucille Gaziano Kennedy for her encouragement and editorial assistance and to Mary Frances Lester for her editorial work on the final manuscript.

—Joe Gulotta

Contents

Foreword

War brings out the worst in human nature. Cruelty and selfishness surface to horrible dimensions, but altruism and love also prevail. Corrie Ten Boom, Maximilian Kolbe and Dietrich Bonhoeffer were among those aspiring to live the Gospel message during World War II. Their witness resulted in imprisonment in Nazi concentration camps.

Corrie Ten Boom was arrested with her father and her sister for sheltering Jews in a secret section of their home. They were subjected to inhumane treatment at the hands of the Nazis. Their father died shortly after his release. Corrie's sister perished in the concentration camp, but Corrie was released because of a clerical error and lived to tell their story.

Maximilian Kolbe was a Franciscan Friar who took another prisoner's place in a starvation bunker. The sadistic commander had arbitrarily selected unfortunate individuals to die agonizing deaths as a punishment for the escapes of other prisoners. Kolbe volunteered because the original victim, a husband and father, pleaded with the Nazis to spare his life. This priest's exemplary behavior merited him eventual canonization as a Saint in the Roman Catholic Church.

Dietrich Bonhoeffer was a successful Protestant minister at the time Hitler was gaining power. Along with other clergymen, Pastor Bonhoeffer resisted Hitler's takeover of the churches in Germany. Bonhoeffer left the country for a time, but returned to confront the evils of Naziism. For taking a stand, this valiant clergyman was captured, imprisoned and executed shortly before the end of the War.

Over 26 million pre-born babies have been slaughtered through legal abortion in the United States since the 1973 Roe v. Wade Supreme Court decision. Although this type of child-killing has become, effectively speaking, a part of the way of life in our society, still there are courageous individuals who have resisted this evil. They have sacrificed their private goals, and in some cases their personal freedoms, to counter the death trend.

The Pro-Life Christians described herein are but a reflection of countless believers nationwide who have committed themselves to this cause. Today's Corrie Ten Booms, Dietrich Bonhoeffers and Maximilian Kolbes are residing throughout the country. Like the victims of the Nazis, Pro-Lifers everywhere are risking their freedoms and their lives for the innocent victims of another and far greater holocaust.

I know the author of *Pro-Life Christians* as an activist at the abortion center in Rockford, Illinois operated by the notorious Dr. Ragsdale. This abortuary attracted nationwide publicity by challenging operational restrictions set by the State of Illinois to regulate such facilities. The Ragsdale v. Turnock case was originally destined for the Supreme Court, but was "settled" for political expediency by an Attorney General seeking the governorship of Illinois—who apparently thought he would get the most support from the radical feminists. He got his compromise, but he lost the election.

Author Joe Gulotta knows firsthand about the evils of an abortion mill that has extinguished tens of thousands of innocent lives. He has seen the women in distress who come there seeking the "help" that they are not going to find. He thanks God for those occasional turnarounds that are brought about by frontline activists. Mr. Gulotta has also experienced the threats and the blasphemous and obscene tirades that Pro-Life witnesses are regularly subjected to at the Rockford mill.

But as happens in many cities with such "death facilities," the Ragsdale abortuary has only a few consistently committed soldiers to help defend the yet unborn. Joe Gulotta is one of those in Rockford. But his concern for the cause goes beyond Rockford and has included regional involvement in Chicago and Milwaukee, as well as participation in the 1990 Rally for Life in Washington, D.C. With a global perspective of the movement, Mr. Gulotta has also corresponded with Mother Teresa on behalf of Pro-Life Rescuers.

This book, *Pro-Life Christians*, is based on Joe's knowledge of Pro-Life leaders he respects. He has carefully selected the people to be included in this book (though realizing that there are many others just as worthy). By underscoring specific personalities and ministries, Mr. Gulotta hopes to inspire believers already called to this mission and to encourage others to become involved. I hope and pray that his goal will be realized.

—Joe Scheidler
Pro-Life Action League

Author's Introduction

In May, 1988 I was in the neighborhood of the only abortion clinic in Rockford, Illinois. Ordinarily, I would not have traveled into its vicinity, but several times during this period I needed, by chance, to drive by the abortion clinic, located in the former Turner School building. If picketers had not been present at the time, I would not have been reminded of the particular "trade" practiced within its walls. Otherwise, the Rockford abortion clinic was easy to ignore due to its innocuous appearance within the old school landmark structure.

When Pro-Life friends of mine had previously invited me to picket this clinic, I had responded that protesting abortion was "not my ministry." However, after I had made three or four attempts at denial, God convicted me. I could no longer call myself a Christian if I continued to look the other way.

Since I secured my first picket sign on that day in May, 1988, I have become a regular at this abortuary. In attending seminars, rallies and protests I have had the privilege of becoming acquainted with many of the Pro-Lifers who are mentioned in this book. I have learned that even the most militant of these people stand for more than the cause of "anti-abortion." They care about the victimized would-be mothers, the fathers, our society and humanity in general.

August, 1990 was another turning point in my Pro-Life involvement. A 64-year-old Milwaukee, Wisconsin grandmother was found guilty of a February, 1989 "Rescue" in Rockford. She was the first person scheduled to be tried for one or both of two local sit-ins, the second one having occurred in April, 1989. ("Rescues" are direct interventions at abortion mills in an effort to save lives peacefully. Those arrested at "Rescues" are attempting to uphold God's law, "Thou shalt not kill," rather than honor man's "law" in the form of the present Supreme Court decision by "right" of which abortions presently take place with seeming legality. For further information on Rescues see the Randall Terry profile in Chapter 11.)

I had previously been arrested in out-of-state Rescue operations, but I was not on trial locally. However, some of the Rockford Pro-Lifers were close friends of mine, and I considered all of them brothers and sisters in the Lord. I desired to be as supportive as possible of them and decided to be an advocate for them. Subsequently, I wrote a letter to Mother Teresa, requesting that she contact the local State's Attorney, asking him to dismiss charges against the remaining Rescuers. I sent my letter on August 17, 1990, which was almost immediately after the Milwaukee grandmother had been sentenced.

I was very grateful that Mother Teresa honored my request, considering her busy schedule as head of an order serving the poor and needy throughout the world. Mother Teresa's letter was a dramatic example of the unity in the Pro-Life movement. Her efforts confirmed that Pro-Lifers are virtually "family" for one another—as well as for the pre-born.

Pro-Life Christians is a book about this caring family. It is composed of life sketches of a cross-section of many of the leading people engaged in this cause. Their approaches and methods may vary. Not all agree on strategies or tactics. For example, Randall Terry and Joan (Andrews) Bell have prayerfully used confrontational measures; whereas, Carol

Everett chooses to use facts and persuasion rather than confrontation. Joe Scheidler boldly attacks abortion directly; whereas, Mary Cunningham Agee concentrates on providing practical alternatives to abortion.

Diverse walks of life are represented by the people chronicled in this book. Julie Makimaa is a housewife, Cyrus Zal is an attorney, James Hickey is a sheriff, and Dr. Willke is a physician.

With all their differences, these individuals have two things in common: they are Christians, and they are dedicated to the pre-born. In writing this book, I hope that the story of their commitment will be an inspiration to Pro-Lifers everywhere, so that they in turn will continue the battle for life which they are waging in their own communities and spheres of influence. I pray that all those fighting for the sanctity of life will be truly awed by what is being done by the believers in Pro-Life portrayed in this book. It is my fond hope that when readers look at the broader picture of the Pro-Life movement, as illustrated here, they will be even more encouraged to continue their own work.

I also hope that Christians not yet called to this movement will be motivated to action by the courageous examples recorded here and by the truth about abortion demonstrated in these pages.

In addition, *this text is intended to be a source of information about the Pro-Life programs mentioned here for the use of anyone interested in joining them or who may wish to be helped by them.*

Pro-Life Christians is by no means intended to contain a complete biography of the individuals profiled; rather, this book emphasizes more the involvement of the various persons in the Pro-Life movement than their life backgrounds, except where this information is related to their efforts to save babies.

Finally, this book is not intended to be all-inclusive in its presentation; indeed, there are many other great Pro-Life leaders who could have been included. Their not being mentioned here is by no means meant as a disparagement of their invaluable work.

—Joe Gulotta

PRO-LIFE
CHRISTIANS

The former Joan Andrews on the day of her wedding to Christopher Bell. Also pictured are Joan's niece and nephew, who made their First Communion on the same day. Joan has since given birth to a beautiful infant girl. Joan continues to be a strong supporter of the Rescue movement.

1

Joan (Andrews) Bell

Possibly the most famous of the Pro-Life Christians of recent years is Joan Bell—formerly Joan Andrews, who has been in prison numerous times because of her courageous work in "Rescue" operations in various parts of the country. (See Chapter 11 for information on Operation Rescue.) Born in 1948 in Tennessee, Joan married Christopher Bell in October, 1991. Joan gave birth to a beautiful, healthy infant girl on September 18, 1992. This daughter was given the name Mary Louise Bell.

As a single woman, Joan sacrificed much of her adult life either by directly working to prevent abortion or by enduring imprisonment because of her work in saving the pre-born. She has rescued babies by courageously placing herself physically between the mother planning to abort and the killing physician, as well as by severing the cord on the doctor's death apparatus.

A devout Roman Catholic, Joan is known throughout the world for her Pro-Life commitment to rescuing the pre-born. She shares the story of her love for these children in the book *You Reject Them, You Reject Me: The Prison Letters of Joan Andrews,* by Richard Cowden Guido. This book can be considered a "Rescue manual." It inspired many people to participate in Rescues, among them Bishop Vaughan.

In a book by John Cavanaugh-O'Keefe, Joan relates how her conscience was moved by the legalization of abortion:

> In 1973, when Roe v. Wade was decided, I was shocked. I felt that we had returned to the world of Nazi Germany. I had always figured that we lived in a civilized world, but now that had changed. I remember that even as a child, I was really horrified by the Nazis. I think I would say I was actually traumatized by learning about what they had done. That such brutality and slaughter could happen in a country that had been Christian, that we called Christian, was shocking...So when I heard about Roe v. Wade, I decided I had to do something.[1]

After lobbying state legislatures, Joan began to intervene directly in order to interrupt the abortion process. For her total dedication to saving the pre-born, Joan has suffered severely. Before "rescuing" became widely known, she had blocked abortuary entrances with only a handful of other Pro-Lifers, sometimes being physically abused in the process. As an example, she was dropped by police while being carried away from one Rescue.[2]

Joan has also endured long, harsh jail sentences for her life-saving activities. Judges, including those with religious backgrounds, tend to obey the letter of man's law during Rescue trials rather than the spirit of God's law. They are apparently "going overboard" to prove that their "personal religious beliefs" are not interfering with their legal rulings.

Joan is committed to non-violence and to love in her Rescue activities. She refuses to cooperate with a legal system that sanctions child-killing. She maintains that "Jesus did not cooperate with evil."[3]

During her prison sentence in Florida, Joan endured months of solitary confinement for attempting to save babies by severing the cord on an abortion suction machine. She was enclosed in a small space with no windows and could take only a few steps. Prison authorities displayed hostility toward Joan because of her refusal to cooperate with them. With deep faith in Jesus Christ and devotion to the Blessed Virgin Mary, she survived this trauma without emotional damage. Joan also felt the prayers of other Pro-Lifers sustaining her.[4]

This author had the privilege of meeting Joan Andrews in Chicago in the Fall of 1990. He was impressed by her humility, her sincerity and her love for the pre-born. In addition, she encourages care and support for pregnant mothers. This "guardian angel" of the weakest and the tiniest human beings believes that "no woman really wants a dead baby, because it is against nature."[5]

Joan affirms her belief in the Rescue process. She contends that without it, the issue of pre-born children who are killed remains a mere issue. However, with this type of saving intervention, abortion rightly becomes known publicly as a life-and-death matter.[6]

Joan further asserts that someone needs to say "No" to abortion. Her warning to pro-aborters is, "You are going to have to do it over my body."[7]

Admitting that society is suffering from other ills, such as poverty, she is nonetheless committed to the pre-born because "they are holocaust victims, and abortion is institutionalized murder."[8]

Joan urges all Pro-Lifers to spend some time at the abortuaries. Children scheduled for execution are being fatally rejected. However, because of the presence of Pro-Lifers outside the killing centers, the pre-born will have been at least shown some love before they die. She encourages activists by stating that God is not concerned with their success, but only with their faithfulness.[9]

Joan had just been released from jail in Youngstown, Ohio shortly before this chapter was originally written. She remains faithful to seeking the "heart of God" in rescuing babies, and because she is a deeply caring person, she prays for all those who pray for her.[10]

While she was in prison in Florida, Joan wrote a letter to Fellow Rescuers which she says best reflects her thoughts and feelings about the Rescue movement. She wrote

> We can never get discouraged as long as we serve the Lord. As long as we do our part, we know He will do His. . .Whatever happens, we can rejoice. I don't think I have ever been happier in my life. . .
>
> Victory in this struggle to end the holocaust is not going to be easy, nor pain free. . .And the victory to come probably will not be soon. I am sure there will be much suffering first. But, oh, thank God we have finally realized this and are all of us taking up the cross we must help each other to bear. This is a reason for great, great joy, for we are committing ourselves to God's work regardless of the cost. . .Therefore, the most important step has already been taken. The rest is in God's hands. . .
>
> I see our people letting go more and more, growing spiritually. . .I believe our new growth is that we realize we must suffer, deeply so, and allow God to be in control, and thus I can see we are trusting Him more completely than ever before. That is why no one should feel badly for me. I am so happy. . .I love and admire all of you so much. Please know that I am with you in prayer and in spirit. . .God bless you, and Mary keep you in her care.—Joan Andrews.[11]

Along with Joan Andrews, the author also had the honor of meeting Chet Gallagher, a former Las Vegas policeman. Mr. Gallagher was discharged from his job because he valiantly stood in support of 92 Rescuers in January, 1989. He has since worked in Rescues with Joan across the country. Chet feels blessed that his last act as a policeman was to save a baby after a mother had changed her mind about having an abortion.[12]

Three happy mothers—Joan (Andrews) Bell at right, with her sisters Susan and Miriam—all due in early October 1992. A triple Baptism by Cardinal O'Connor is planned.

2
Julie Makimaa

In 1962 Lee Kinney, a 17-year-old girl, moved from the slums of Philadelphia to San Francisco with her mother and sisters to escape family beatings from an alcoholic father. Determined to forge a new life for herself, she secured an office job.

One of the employees invited Lee to what he said was a pizza party. To her utter dismay, this naive teenager found herself to be the only guest. The host, who was a man 20 years her senior, had cancelled with everyone except her. The whole event was a charade to trap her. Within a short period of time, he had brutally raped her.

Shocked and frightened, Lee had no place to turn. In 1963, there were no rape hotlines, and victims were almost always blamed for the crime. To avert further humiliation, Lee did not contact the police. Her trauma was later compounded when she discovered that she was pregnant.

A friend encouraged Lee to have an abortion and advised her: "Lee, you don't deserve this." At that time, abortion was illegal and meant a trip outside the United States for a dangerous procedure.

With abortion, therefore, not an option, she moved in with an elderly couple in Los Angeles until she had her baby. Lee was not allowed to see or hold her infant girl at birth because

6

she had earlier decided to release her child for adoption. It was believed that separation would be easier if the new mother had no contact with the baby after the delivery.

Her daughter, Julie Anderson, grew up in California until her family moved to northern Michigan when she was 15. At age seven, Julie learned that she was adopted; this news came from a friend who had overheard this fact in a conversation between their respective parents. Julie's playmate was trying to get even during an argument by divulging this secret.

Julie always believed that her adoptive parents loved her, but a curiosity about her natural parents occasionally stirred in her mind. Feeling that her adoptive parents were her "real parents," Julie did not seriously begin searching for her natural parents until after her marriage to Bob Makimaa.

After three and a half years and many phone calls and letters, Julie noticed a telephone number on one of the hospital birth records. Dialing it bore fruit. After 20 years, it was still in service and belonged to the aging couple who had mercifully sheltered a frightened pregnant teenager named Lee Kinney in 1963. Because Lee kept in touch with them, Mr. and Mrs. Croft, the elderly couple, knew her whereabouts. However, Mrs. Croft initially refused to assist Julie in finding Lee. Julie persisted and wrote a letter to the Crofts. After holding this letter for two weeks and praying for guidance, they phoned Lee and read it to her. Lee called Julie the following morning.

In their first conversation, Julie and her mother, who was now Lee Ezell since her marriage, discovered that they both had a deep faith in the Lord Jesus. Divine Providence had guided these women to each other after two decades of separation. They were elated and decided to meet in eight weeks. For Julie, it seemed like almost an eternity.

After six weeks, Lee's husband phoned the Makimaa's and informed Julie that he wanted to talk with her husband. Julie was filled with anxiety as she pondered this unexpected turn of events.

Lee's husband told Bob that Julie had been conceived through a sexual assault and left the decision to Bob as to whether Julie should be informed of this. After Bob revealed the facts of the conversation to Julie, she felt very blessed to be alive, regardless of her beginnings.

However, Julie's concern was for Lee. She wondered why her natural mother would ever want to meet her. Fearful that she would be a reminder of that terrible experience years before, Julie did not think that Lee would contact her again.

After much anticipation by Julie, Lee phoned her to confirm the reunion plans. Julie was overjoyed that her mother still wanted to meet her. With deep compassion for her mother, Julie asked Lee why she was willing to continue the reunion, considering the nature of Julie's conception.

Lee shared the fact that she had healed emotionally from the rape experience and that she felt no connection between that traumatic event and their reunion. Julie was more elated than ever as they made final plans.

The two were finally united, along with their spouses, in adjoining motel rooms in Washington, D.C., where they celebrated Julie's 21st birthday. Although Julie had previously received a photo of Lee, when they met, she marvelled at their resemblance. The first words uttered by Julie's husband to Lee were, "I want to thank you for not aborting Julie; I don't know what my life would be without her and my daughter." All present became more acquainted as Lee related the experiences of Julie's conception and birth.

The reunion was just the beginning for Julie and Lee. Since that time, they have combined forces, along with Julie's husband, to speak out for pre-born babies conceived through rape and for their victim mothers. Julie and Lee have appeared on *The Sally Jessy Raphael Show, Geraldo, Attitudes, The 700 Club, 100 Huntley Street,* and *Sonia Live.* In addition, *Focus on the Family, Prime Time America, Open Line,* and *Point of View* have broadcast their message of compassion via radio. Lee is author of the book, *The Missing*

Piece (published by Bantam), which portrays her personal experiences.

Although Julie and Lee have developed a close working relationship, Julie wants to make this point clear: Some adoptive parents who hear her story believe that she discarded her relationship with her own adoptive parents after finding her natural mother. Therefore, every time she shares her experience, she states that her relationship with her adoptive parents is still good and that no one will ever be able to replace them. They are her Mom and Dad.

Julie founded Fortress International, an organization to work with and for women who become pregnant through rape or incest and for children conceived by these acts. In describing Fortress International, Julie declares, "We at Fortress want to let women, children and their families know that there are people who care and understand. We are not trained counselors, but are people who have been personally affected by a sexual assault pregnancy, and are willing to be there for women and children who have been through similar situations."

Fortress International helps pregnant victims of sexual assault to find alternatives to abortion, for the sake of both mothers and their children. Compassionate members of this organization throughout the nation personally reach out with encouragement and understanding to those who are hurting. They also make appropriate referrals to crisis pregnancy centers and qualified professionals.

Dispelling myths about sexual assault is central to Julie's mission. As an example, a common argument for legalized abortion is that rape victims should be allowed to terminate their pregnancies. This implies that a child conceived through sexual assault is evil and does not deserve to live. The truth is that the child is innocent, just like his or her mother.

Another misconception is that a mother will never be able to love a child conceived by rape or incest. Quite the contrary; Julie maintains that "The child is the only good thing that can result from such a devastating act" and that mothers who conceive because of rape or incest do love their children who are born out of such traumatic beginnings.

Although many people believe that few or no pregnancies result from sexual assault, the fact is that this is more common than is generally assumed. And given the magnitude of the problem, all the victims involved require help.

Julie also confronts the myth that women are somehow responsible for sexual assault with the fact that they are usually innocent victims. Furthermore, she advocates that penalties be more severe for the real criminals—the rapists.

With the assistance of David Reardon, author of *Aborted Women: Silent No More,* Fortress International is conducting a national survey to assess the needs of those who have had sexual assault pregnancies. The results will be used to inform the public and develop necessary programs for the victims. Fortress International can be contacted by writing to: P.O. Box 7352, Springfield, IL 62791-7352 or by phoning 217-529-9545. This organization also welcomes financial support, which is much needed and is tax deductible.

Julie has been a key person in testifying before the Louisiana Legislature to promote the passing of a Pro-Life bill that will protect *all* children, no matter under what circumstances they were conceived. She believes that the unwillingness of the Pro-Life movement to stand firm in the cases of rape and incest pregnancies has forestalled ultimate victory. She maintains that pro-abortionists purposely use the rape-incest issue to fight back with every time Pro-Lifers try to take away their "right to abortion."

Julie declares:

> In order to win this issue, we must be compassionate to the woman who has been assaulted, and at the same time defend the life of the innocent child that has been conceived. If we truly believe that life begins at conception, then we cannot for any reason allow

a compromise that will permit the intentional killing of children whose fathers were criminals.

Julie doubts that she would be alive today, let alone her two children, if her mother had had access to a legal abortion. Consequently, in a spirit of gratitude, she is doing all she can to insure that other children who have been conceived as she was may someday rejoice in the fact that they too are alive.

If Julie had not been born, her husband would have been deprived of the wonderful spouse whom the Lord destined for him. The Pro-Life community would also have been without a champion who heroically espouses the cause of sexually assaulted women and children. Who would ever have guessed that a violent sexual assault in 1963 would result in one of the strongest cases against abortion in instances of rape and incest—the case of a living human being who loves God and her own life?

The story of Lee Ezell and Julie Makimaa is a confirmation of the Scripture passage, "We know that to them that love God, all things work together unto good, to such as, according to his purpose, are called to be saints." (*Rom.* 8:28).

Julie Makimaa (right), who was conceived through rape, and her mother Lee Ezell. Mother and daughter were joyfully reunited when Julie was 21. Julie founded Fortress International to support women and children involved in conceptions from rape and incest.

3
Gianna Jessen

Gianna Jessen's life is no less than a miracle. This talented singer and speaker survived a saline-solution abortion, although she had been pronounced dead by medical personnel after the procedure.

Speaking in various places both in the United States and abroad, this bubbly young lady (15 years old at this writing) spreads a message of love and forgiveness. She even understands the desperation which her natural mother must have experienced at age 17 when she decided to abort Gianna.

Gianna's best argument against abortion is her story about her "miracle" birth. She declares, "Somebody tried to murder me—no doubt about it!" Then she adds, "God stepped in with another plan. Now, I'm spreading God's word."

Although Gianna was pronounced dead after undergoing a procedure that usually burns the baby on the inside and outside, a nurse noted that she was still alive and took her to a hospital. Her condition was so serious that she could not move, but could only lie there "like a piece of cooked spaghetti." Doctors repeatedly declared she would not live and that efforts to rehabilitate her would be futile. But *they* were wrong; she *did* live and she is still alive today!

The second "miracle" came when three-year-old Gianna was taken in by a Christian foster parent who was determined that she would have a happy and productive life. Her foster mother worked with her until she learned to walk—after physicians had predicted that she would never be able to walk. Gianna believes that "God is more powerful than doctors!"

In addition to learning to walk, Gianna also has had to learn to live with cerebral palsy. However, she feels that she is basically no different from other people, even though she has a disability. Among the activities she enjoys are hiking and youth theater in her home state of California.

Gianna was adopted into a Christian home and has come to know through her own remarkable birth and life that "You are really lost if you don't have Jesus in your life." She maintains that those who provide counseling at abortion-center entrances and those who participate in Rescues to save pre-born babies are "special to God and to me." Gianna herself has taken part in anti-abortion protests, including a Rescue in Atlanta.

Gianna's message is one of hope and love. She does not condemn women who have had abortions, but she works to help prevent situations which could lead to future abortions.

She relates well to other young people and recognizes that being a teenager is not easy today, especially when the mass media encourages a casual approach to pre-marital sex. Believing sex before marriage is not good for young people, she encourages them to wait. Gianna assures teens, "There is a plan" in waiting.

Perhaps Gianna's greatest gift is her voice, which she uses to convey hope. Through her musical talent, Gianna reaches out with the Pro-Life message of love for the pre-born.

Gianna Jessen, now a beautiful young girl, began her life by surviving a saline abortion. Today she brings a joyful Pro-Life Christian message to audiences worldwide.

4

Carol Everett

Although abortion physicians and clinic managers may claim to care for women, this is really far from the truth. Pro-Lifers point out that the profit motive is the primary driving force behind this death industry. The accusation is confirmed by a reliable source of information on the subject—former abortionists themselves. A bold witness to this truth of the gruesome trade of abortion is Carol Everett, once director of the most successful abortion clinic in Dallas, Texas, and a woman who had sold 35,000 abortions.[1] According to Carol, business was so booming that her income had risen to nearly $15,000 per month and she planned to expand to five clinics, anticipating earnings of as much as one million dollars a year.[2] Carol's dream was to be the "leading lady" in the abortion industry. She even initiated her 14-year-old daughter into the business.

However, with the prayers and help of a Christian pastor, she experienced a profound conversion around 1983 and has since become a Pro-Life advocate. Burning now with an evangelical zeal, Carol preaches her message in travels throughout the nation. Speaking to Pro-Life groups, she asks them to unite in prayer to halt the calamity of abortion.

Carol believes in her message so profoundly that she appeared before the Texas State Legislature to plead for an end to abortion-on-demand. Many of her former associates in the abortion business were present to hear her denounce this practice and to affirm her new direction.

Present at a 1988 Rockford, Illinois talk, this author heard Carol courageously share her own personal tragedy—her abortion, one consequence of which was that her marriage ended in divorce. This is only one case showing that abortion can be extremely destructive to marital relationships—as well as being virtually always fatal to the child.

She also revealed the devious techniques which clinic "counselors" use to convince women that abortion is the best choice. Fear is instilled into the victims in order to scare them into killing their pre-born children. For instance, the "counselor" may capitalize on dread of the baby's father or the would-be mother's parents' knowing about the pregnancy. Of course, abortion is offered as the solution to a crisis pregnancy; it is presented as the best and easiest way to eliminate a distressful predicament.

The fact that a clinic worker would refer to the father as the "father" is contradictory, according to Carol. For in the conversation with the mother, this death salesperson in all likelihood would assure her that the child in her womb was only a "blob," or just a "tissue that she was having eliminated," rather than a baby. Since a blob or tissue cannot have a father, this line of reasoning exemplifies an obvious deception on the part of clinic "counselors."

Integral to the "counseling" procedure is the assurance of payment from the would-be mother. Carol divulged some of the strategies used to secure the full amount. Persuading an underaged girl to work a part-time job or to borrow small amounts of money from a number of friends was identified as a common approach.[3] Of course, abortionists oppose parental-consent laws, which would decrease the number of abortions performed, and subsequently their revenue.

According to this former clinic director, the entire payment is always demanded, to the last penny. No abortion will be performed without it! "It's not to help women," she charges; "it's a business." Physicians can routinely perform from 10 to 12 first-trimester abortions an hour, with some doing even more. Their cut is about one third of the fee. For example, a $250 killing procedure will result in $75 in blood money for the abortionist. In a second or third-trimester abortion, the price on the head of the baby can go up to $8,000, with the doctor pocketing 50%. Since a part-time abortionist, working an 18-hour week, can make $45,000 a month in cash,[4] there should be no wonder that the pro-abortion lobbying forces are well-financed and are determined to continue to keep child-killing legal.

In order to guarantee an ample supply of unsuspecting young mothers, Carol got involved in high-school sex-education programs. Using a devious strategy, she would invite students to her clinic, where she would provide them with low-dose birth control pills having a high rate of pregnancy in order to promote promiscuity, more pregnancies and more abortion business. The goal was three to five abortions per girl between 13 and 18 years of age.[5]

Carol tells how she kept a Bible in her desk drawer to pull out when anyone would say that abortion is a sin. Carol would reply, "I am helping women because God wants me to." Carol tithed religiously. Incredibly, she says, "I even believed God was blessing me in the abortion industry because of my tithe..."[6]

Pregnancy testing by abortion clinics is traumatic, since their results, according to Carol, are almost always positive. "There are times when the patient isn't pregnant at all," she declares.

Attacking a common myth, Carol asserts that a baby being aborted *can* feel pain during the procedure. At six weeks of development, the fetus has a heart and all other body parts. In addition, the mother can feel pain during the killing of her baby, and abortion, she maintains, can be excruciatingly painful.

Drawing from her own abortion experience, Carol warns that a mother will feel the results of her action the rest of her life. The psychological effects of abortion are known as post-abortion syndrome. Its symptoms include depression, which may lead to drug abuse, alcoholism, self-destructive behavior and/or sexual promiscuity. Other family relationships are often affected by abortion. The healing process after an abortion must begin with the mother's acknowledgment of the fact that she has killed her baby.

According to Carol Everett, "Everything about abortion is based on a lie!" To turn the tide on this child-killing, she advocates prayer. She believes it to be a powerful source of conversion, and she encourages prayer outside of abor?tuaries.

As a Christian, Carol Everett exhorts Pro-Lifers to adhere to the doctrine of love in relating to abortionists and their victims. She reminds us, "We love the sinner, not the sin."

This author was also present at the April, 1990 Rally for Life in Washington, D. C., where Carol Everett addressed hundreds of thousands of people. In an interview recorded on the Rally video, *Tell the Truth,* she maintains that abortion is not safe. In her last 18 months in the abortion business, she observed that about one in 500 women either died or required major surgery, such as a hysterectomy or a colostomy, due to a perforated uterus sustained as a result of an abortion.

Carol Everett is a truly *powerful* witness for the Pro-Life movement because of having undergone an abortion herself and because of her former role in the abortion business. By telling the truth boldly about this nefarious trade, she is com?bating the deceptions perpetrated by the lucrative death industry.

Carol's organization, Life Network, is located in Dallas, Texas. A convincing speaker, she is available upon request to give her message directly to groups or by radio or televi?sion. As an example of her willingness to speak whenever and wherever she can, she recently shared her experiences on Dr. James Dobson's *Focus on the Family* radio program, which is broadcast on over 1,500 stations daily.

Carol shares a detailed account of her story in her 1991 autobiography *The Scarlet Lady: Confessions of a Successful Abortionist* (Wolgemuth & Hyatt, Publishers, Inc.). She describes how childhood problems contributed to her decision to enter the death industry. In addition, Carol gives a full account of her abortion and divorce, her drive to become the "leading lady" in the business and her downfall as an abortionist. The text ends with an encouraging theme as she describes her conversion and her Pro-Life activities.

Carol Everett, who used to run the most successful abortion clinic in Dallas—in addition to having had an abortion herself. Today Carol exposes her former occupation as a cold-blooded, deceitful, lucrative, unregulated industry.

5
Cindi Guasto

Those promoting abortion have often sold it as a safe, noon-hour type procedure, with minimal physical and/or emotional risks to the would-be mother. However, an increasing number of sources have contested this claim, citing evidence that abortion is dangerous to the women involved.

As mentioned in the previous chapter, former abortion-clinic manager Carol Everett observed in her business that about one in 500 women either died from or required major surgery after an abortion. In addition, post-abortion syndrome (PAS) is becoming recognized as an emotional consequence of abortion. PAS consists of a constellation of symptoms, which can be immediate or delayed—even by 10 or 15 years (or more) after an abortion.

As an example, Dr. Anne Speckhard, Ph.D. conducted a study on the long-term effects of abortion. Using a small sample of 30 women exhibiting high-stress reactions to their abortions, Dr. Speckhard discovered that these reactions occurred even after 5 to 10 years. As a sample of her findings:

81% were preoccupied with thoughts of the aborted child.
73% experienced flashbacks to the abortion experience.
69% had feelings of "craziness" after the abortion.

54% had nightmares related to the abortion.
35% experienced "visitations" from the aborted child.
23% had hallucinations related to the abortion.

Her study is called *Psycho-Social Stress following Abortion* and was published by Sheed and Ward in 1987.

Although their backgrounds varied, these women had consistent reactions. Seventy-two percent of them claimed that they had had no religious beliefs before the abortion, but afterwards they considered abortion to be the taking of a human life—in other words, a murder.

If Dr. Speckhard's study is in any way representative of the approximately 26 million abortions performed since 1973, many women in our country need help to be healed psychologically and/or emotionally.

Cindi was one of these "walking wounded." An unwed mother at 17 years of age, Cindi married and bore her first child. She became pregnant again and aborted. She reasoned that it was better to end her pregnancy than to bring another child into a troubled marriage.

Cindi had no remorse for 14 years after her abortion. However, while anticipating the birth of her grandson, she became depressed and tearful for no apparent reason. She was remarried, to Frank Guasto, who did not initially understand her emotions.

Cindi began thinking about her abortion. She wondered about her aborted baby's physical characteristics, such as his or her sex, eye color and height, in addition to the personal preferences and tastes he would have had in music, sports and hobbies.

Guilt and remorse surfaced in her as the birth of her grandchild neared, although she ultimately rejoiced after the delivery. Developing a close bond with her grandson made Cindi wish that she had not aborted her second child. She frequently wondered what it would have been like to be with the baby she had aborted.

Acknowledging the wrong she had done, Cindi repented and experienced God's forgiveness and healing. Out of her conversion, she developed a desire to assist other women with problem pregnancies.

Today she is a volunteer at the Northern Illinois Crisis Pregnancy Center in Rockford, Illinois. This is one of the many organizations nationwide that assist women with emotional, physical and spiritual problems as a result of their having had abortions—as well as providing free pregnancy testing and counseling to help pregnant women choose life. The center uses the excellent video, *Window to the Womb,* which gives an ultrasound view of the pre-born child as he moves around inside his mother. Maternity clothing and baby items are also available for women who come to the Crisis Pregnancy Center.

Because of her own abortion experience, Cindi is able genuinely to empathize with her clients. She receives satisfaction from knowing that she is helping them to choose life for their babies. To those who are in agony from Post-Abortion Syndrome, Cindi offers understanding and emotional support to facilitate their healing process.

Having given deep encouragement to his wife during her trauma, Cindi's husband Frank has also dedicated himself to this cause. Frank is a member of the Board of Directors of the Northern Illinois Crisis Pregnancy Center, and his mission is to promote awareness of its services in the local community. According to Frank and Cindi:

> We are trying to do something as an alternative to abortion. The pro-death forces say, "Yes, you are against abortion, but what are you doing to help girls in need?" Our answer is the open door of the CPC, where caring, concern and the love of Christ are presented. It's our ultimate endeavor to lead girls in crisis to Christ. This is the ultimate and the only lasting answer to eliminating the abortion holocaust.

Cindi Guasto and her husband, Frank. Cindi had an abortion as a young woman of about 18. Fourteen years later she was hit with poignant sorrow and remorse. Cindi made peace with God and now counsels women at the Northern Illinois Crisis Pregnancy Center.

6

Sheriff James Hickey

According to Dante, "The hottest places in Hell are reserved for those who, having the power and responsibility to oppose evil, did nothing to extinguish it." If Dante is correct in this, is then the opposite also true: that is, does God reward with the highest places in Heaven those who resist evil at a great price to themselves? Hopefully, this is true. And Sheriff James Hickey of Corpus Christi, Texas is such an individual.

The fifth generation of a south Texas pioneer family, Sheriff Hickey exemplifies in himself the traditional Christian values of hard work, honesty and personal honor. He attributes his character formation to his parents and to his high-school education by the Benedictine Fathers.

Sheriff Hickey's professional credentials are numerous and impressive, since he has distinguished himself in business and in public service. With his exceptional qualifications and accomplishments, his is a success story in a culture which places a high premium on personal success.

However, Sheriff Hickey differs from most who have reached the pinnacle of their careers and who concentrate on maintaining their positions. He has decided to seek heavenly treasures, rather than to strive for earthly ones. In an extraordinary act of courage, he has refused to assist city police in arresting participants in local Rescue operations if called upon to do so.

Rescues are designed to save lives; they consist in Pro-Lifers' peacefully placing their bodies between the expectant mothers and the abortuary entrances. These acts of "civil disobedience" are direct interventions aimed at preventing child-killing—as distinct from demonstrations on the sidewalks in front of abortuaries, which are generally non-confrontational by comparison.

Obedient to the Scriptural mandate from *Acts* 4:19, Sheriff Hickey's motto is, "My first duty is to God—His law comes first." Because of his conviction that abortion is actually baby-killing, he declares, "Nobody has the responsibility to enforce an unjust law." Going a step further, Sheriff Hickey offers prayer support during Rescues. With 23 years of service in law enforcement, this veteran officer has incurred criticism from pro-abortion groups and from law-enforcement organizations. In addition, the American Civil Liberties Union has threatened to sue him for displaying Pro-Life posters in his office.

Scheduled for re-election in 1992, Sheriff Hickey has unselfishly placed his reputation and his career on the line, distinguishing himself as a man of great moral fortitude. Honored by the area's Body of Christ Rescue organization for his Pro-Life commitment, he is an outstanding witness for the Gospel of Jesus Christ. The publicity generated by his position also keeps the local slaughter in public view, thereby pricking people's consciences.

Sheriff Hickey likens the legalization of abortion to the segregation laws of the 1960's, or to the killing of Jews in Nazi Germany. He believes that the 1973 Roe v. Wade decision, legalizing abortion, will eventually be overturned, because it is immoral. In the meantime, he plans to continue to do his best to protect the pre-born.

Sheriff Hickey's first wife, Sylvia, who died in 1986, was also a devoted Pro-Lifer. He is remarried to a Pro-Life woman named Jan, also an active Rescuer. In a team effort, Sheriff Hickey has prayed at a Rescue while his wife blocked the entrance.

The object of controversy, he nonetheless possesses the moral character needed for the job of law enforcement. With a history of corruption and scandals in government, this nation is blessed to have the likes of James Hickey in a position of such authority. We need more individuals in public office who will stand for right moral principles, instead of acting for political expediency and self-gain. Grouping abortion with pornography and drug abuse, Sheriff Hickey identifies them as "symptoms of great national illnesses."

Since the strength of a nation is built upon men of courage, a defeat of Sheriff Hickey at the ballot box would only further weaken a nation that is in a moral decline.

According to a story in the Corpus Christi *Caller-Times,* Corpus Christi Bishop Rene Gracida counselled his flock to vote for Sheriff Hickey in 1992. The Pro-Life community in Corpus Christi is a tribute to God's people working together to counteract an evil. Here is a case where a law enforcement chief, a religious leader and the local Pro-Life organizations support each other in a united effort to save pre-born babies. In this respect, Corpus Christi serves as a shining example for cities everywhere, showing how prominent people can promote life and help allow babies to be born.

Sheriff Hickey, at the forefront of the Corpus Christi movement, is known as a humble man who gives the glory to God and the credit to those who taught him sound religious doctrine.

Sheriff James Hickey of Corpus Christi, Texas, who courageously refuses to assist city police in arresting Rescuers at local abortion mills. Sheriff Hickey states, "My first duty is to God—His law comes first."

7

Doctor James Dobson

In this era of abortion on demand, New-Age theologies, occult practices, valueless values, values-clarification curricula, permissive sex education and secular humanism, psychologist Dr. James Dobson, with his *Focus on the Family* radio program, is a champion of pro-family ideals for Christians of all denominations. A minister's son, Dr. Dobson offers the Gospel of Jesus Christ as an alternative to modern-day worldly psychologies[1] on over 1,500[2] radio stations.

His broadcasts cover subjects that encompass the entire range of human problems and needs. From child-rearing to death and dying, from money management to mental health, from saving pre-born babies to saving marriages, Dr. Dobson touches deeply virtually every aspect of our existence. However, as a zealous Pro-Life advocate, Dr. Dobson's passion for justice is inflamed by this cause more than by any other.

Dr. Dobson's strong sentiments on abortion are quoted in *Turning Hearts Toward Home* by Rolf Zettersten:

> Is there any fundamental difference between a baby who resides in his mother's uterus and one who has made an eight-inch journey down the birth canal?. . . Surely the Lord does not look upon the baby inside the uterus with any less love and concern than one

who enters the world a few minutes later. The only difference between them is that one can be seen and the other cannot...It is true that law recognizes a different status for those born versus those unborn, but the law in this instance is wrong.[3]

Dr. Dobson compares the holocaust of abortion to the killing of Jews and other prisoners in the Nazi extermination camps of World War II. With over 26 million babies killed by abortion in the U.S.A. from 1973 to date, he believes that this horror will someday be recognized to be as obvious as that of the Nazis.[4]

One of the main speakers at the April, 1990 Rally for Life in Washington, D. C., he inspired hundreds of thousands of people by predicting victory for the Pro-Life movement. This, he said, will be in spite of what he called a "love affair between the media and the pro-abortion movement"[5] and the fact that the pro-abortion factions hold considerable power.[6]

In his historic presentation at the nation's capital, Dr. Dobson compared abortion-on-demand to the American Civil War, when brother fought brother. Similar to that bloody conflict, the Pro-Life battle will not be fought from the safety of people's living rooms, according to Dr. Dobson. In addition, he challenged Pro-Life Christians to arouse the same level of commitment as their forefathers did in winning their ferocious battles.

The critical difference, he said, is that the Pro-Life conflict is waged without deadly guns or grenades or on traditional military battlefields. Dr. Dobson targeted three areas where we have to defeat abortion:

First: The ballot box, where voters can express their views to politicians, especially to those who have deserted the Pro-Life camp for political expediency. "Where are the statesmen?" he asked, suggesting it may be time to "retire" some of the politicians.[7]

Second: The public schools, which he said need to be

returned to parental authority. He described the National Education Association as a "national disaster"[8] and exhorted parents to monitor what children are being taught in school.

Third: The new nominees to the U.S. Supreme Court must be supportive of the Pro-Life position. Voters must be prepared to express their strong sentiments when a vacancy among justices occurs.

Dr. Dobson closed his Washington presentation by declaring that he will never cast a vote for a man or woman who is willing to allow the killing of a single innocent baby.[9]

Dr. Dobson's *Focus on the Family* featured Randall Terry, founder of Operation Rescue, shortly after the massive Washington, D. C. rally. (See the profile on Randall Terry in Chapter 11.) Dr. Dobson dedicated an entire broadcast to the dangers to free speech and religious liberties posed by governmental attempts to break Operation Rescue.[10] While protecting the child-killing industry, prosecuting attorneys and law enforcement agencies and courts have served as instruments of "oppression and tyranny,"[11] according to Mr. Terry. Along with other *Focus* guests, he maintained that Rescuers have received harsh sentences for what are technically only "misdemeanors" (e.g., trespassing and resisting arrest) and have served as the targets of police brutality.[12]

At the same time, Pro-Lifers have usually not been allowed to testify as to their motive for blocking abortuary entrances. The "necessity defense," which overrides trespass laws in situations where human life is in danger, has almost never been recognized in Rescue trials.[13]

Dr. Dobson has devoted more than lip service to the Rescue movement. His own staff members are among those who have laid their bodies down to save their pre-born brothers and sisters and who have been subjected to harsh sentences.[14]

Dr. Dobson has also featured other Pro-Life activists, such as former abortion clinic manager Carol Everett,[15] as well as Lee Ezell, with her daughter Julie Makimaa,[16] who was conceived as a result of rape. (Carol, Lee and Julie are also highlighted in this book. See Chapters 4 and 2 respectively.)

Whether condemning the evil of abortion or promoting the "adoption option," Dr. Dobson is continually exhorting his audience to choose life.

His academic credentials include a doctorate from the University of Southern California in child development. Dr. Dobson distinguished himself as a professor at the University of Southern California Medical School before dedicating his talents to the Lord full-time in 1977. In addition, he served on the Attending Staff of Children's Hospital of Los Angeles in the Division of Child Development and Medical Genetics.[17]

A best-selling author, Dr. Dobson's publications include *Hide or Seek, Dare to Discipline, The Strong-Willed Child, Love Must Be Tough, What Wives Wish Their Husbands Knew About Women,* and *Straight Talk to Men and Their Wives.* He also recently co-authored *Children at Risk* with Gary Bauer. Because he is a voice for sound, traditional values, this Christian psychologist was chosen to serve on the President's Commission on Pornography during the Reagan administration. President George Bush has also consulted Dr. Dobson on family issues.[18]

Dr. Dobson prizes his wife Shirley as his best friend, and he displays his obvious affection when referring to his son Ryan and his daughter Danae. Although his work is vitally important to him, this dedicated husband and father is also focused on his own family as his greatest treasure, next to God.

Dr. James Dobson, famous psychologist who brings Christian pro-family ideals to a huge audience through his books and his *Focus on the Family* radio program. Dr. Dobson is an outspoken defender of the rights of all pre-born children.

8
Father Paul Marx

The United States has suffered tragic consequences from the decline of Judeo-Christian values. Abortion, euthanasia, pornography, sexual promiscuity, AIDS, child abuse and sexual crimes are all the result of the immoral mentality pervasive in our society. We should all thank God for the souls dedicated to fighting these problems and their causes.

However, these abominations have become global, and they threaten family values everywhere in the world, not just in our own country. Because the family was ordained by God to be the framework in which new human beings are born into this world, nurtured and raised to maturity, as well as the institution that sustains parents and children alike, the forces of darkness and deception seek universally to destroy the family structure.

To help counter this global attack on the family, God has raised up Fr. Paul Marx of Human Life International (HLI). Fr. Marx has the distinction of being called "America's Number One Pro-Life Advocate," "the George Washington of the Pro-Life Movement" and the "World's Leading Authority on Pro-Life Matters." He has likely cooperated with more Pro-Life individuals and groups than has any other person, as he spends much of his time traveling around the world— conferring with leaders, gathering information and setting up

34

HLI branch offices in 52 nations. Fr. Marx thus has an extremely valuable overall view of the huge and very organized anti-life forces at work all over the world today. Fr. Marx says: "We need to work internationally, because this is an international Devil's movement."[1]

HLI has four publications: *HLI Reports* (an international monthly Pro-Life family newsletter); a monthly *Special Report* (a fascinating letter detailing Fr. Marx's constant international travels); *Parish and Family Notes* (a monthly for pastors); and *Population Research Institute Review* (a bi-monthly newsletter refuting the contraception imperialists and the overpopulation fanatics).

After 30 years of teaching in the fields of marriage and family life, this Benedictine monk founded the Human Life Center in 1972 at Minnesota's St. John University. He transferred to Washington, D. C. and began Human Life International in 1980, whose offices have since moved to Gaithersburg, Maryland. He started this organization

> because all over the world a war is being waged against God, love, marriage, the family, even life itself. . .Our purpose is to restore and promote Judeo-Christian values. These are values that are real, that last a lifetime, that bring true happiness. . .So we're working to strengthen families, enrich marriages and restore the absolutely crucial place for the family in our society.[2]

Fr. Marx views abortion as the core of an entire cluster of evils caused by the abuse of God's gift of sexuality. He has little faith in most professional or religious people in providing leadership. "They're weakened hopelessly by the values of the world,"[3] according to Fr. Marx.

Furthermore, he believes that the abortion battle is temporarily lost in Europe and in North America. On the other hand, he is optimistic about saving babies in Third World countries, where, he states, 90% of all births take place and where families are still cherished.

This is not to say that Fr. Marx is giving up the fight in the U.S., but he is focusing heavily on underdeveloped nations, which do not have the tools which are available in the West, including films, photos, books and literature. Despite Americans' having these tools, Fr. Marx states,

> the fact is that most Americans still don't know what abortion is. They don't know the consequences of abortion, how it ruins a woman's health, how it means the dying of a nation. As I have seen in 84 countries, abortion, once legalized, makes people very careless with their sexual lives. They say, "We won't get pregnant, and if we do, we can always have a legal abortion." In that way, legal abortion means the destruction of marriage and the family. Today twenty-five percent of Americans were not born here, because we now have a future only by importing people into this country. . . . So abortion also means the destruction of the nation.[4]

Fr. Marx has been one of the few to speak out on the fact that surgical abortion is only the tip of the abortion iceberg. He states that the real figures on the numbers killed in the U.S. are: "1.6 million a year by doctors, and another 8 to 9 million by Pill, IUD, Norplant, Morning-after Pill and so on. . ."[5] These numbers show the true and abominable nation-wide picture of abortion.

From his worldwide vantage point Fr. Marx is uniquely qualified to see the causes of the near-universal crisis in the family. He states that

> contraception always leads to abortion. There is no exception. There is no contracepting society with a nice family life, and with little fornication, adultery,

VD, or divorce. There is no such society anywhere in the world. I have looked for it.[6]

Fr. Marx sees the current state of the world—"with the massive VD out of control, with the infertility levels so high because of sex abuse, with the AIDS threat, with the babies [being] killed"—as proving that "Christianity was always right when it spoke for chastity,"[7] when it said that sexual relations and those actions that lead to sexual relations are for the married alone.

Fr. Marx states that "75% of doctor-done abortions last year [1991] were done on the unmarried. These killings were the outcome of fornication or adultery."[8]

Fr. Marx identifies the International Planned Parenthood Federation as the "number one enemy" of family values throughout the world. "One leading cause of sexual chaos and the abortion holocaust is Planned Parenthood: Their method is always the same: get the people on contraception, and it inevitably leads to abortion, in every country."[9] Fr. Marx also cites other powerful forces working for the same anti-family goals: the population controllers at the United Nations and the U.S. Agency for International Development (USAID).[10]

To attack this "godless monster," Human Life International educates in the following pro-family areas: marriage preparation, marriage enrichment, care of the aged and the infirm, teenage chastity, parent effectiveness training, death and dying counseling, advice on sexuality and love, and information on breast-feeding and natural childbirth—plus on such evils as sex education, sterilization, homosexuality, so-called "death with dignity," suicide and school-based condom distribution.

The centerpiece of HLI's activities is Natural Family Planning (NFP), which allows couples who have a serious reason for avoiding the conception of a child at a particular time to avoid conception without committing a sin; NFP is based on abstinence during the woman's fertile time each month—which can now be determined very accurately. [According to Catholic teaching, Natural Family Planning may not be used simply as a means to avoid children, based only on the personal choice of the couple. It may be used only if 1) Both parties freely agree to the restrictions that it involves; 2) The practice does not constitute an occasion of sin, especially the sin of incontinence; 3) There is a serious reason for not having children, at least for the time being.[11]—*Editor.*]

Fr. Marx is a pioneer of the NFP movement, having begun its promotion in the early 1950's; in 1977 he founded the *International Review of Natural Family Planning.* In addition, he has sponsored 10 international symposia on NFP.

Fr. Marx believes HLI has accomplished "more than we ever dreamed of." Through major international seminars in various cities of the world, HLI teaches members of the healing and helping professions "the latest in natural family planning, how to combat medical violence in all its forms, how to teach young people to be pure, everything that's needed so desperately today."[12] These programs are presented by some of the most outstanding experts in the world who are dedicated to Christian family values.

Thousands of professionals from diverse nations throughout the world have been trained in NFP. These key people carry their knowledge back home and, in turn, train thousands of others. Fr. Marx, who is a "mover and shaker," declares, "That's our whole purpose—to solve problems, not just to state them."[13]

One fruit of HLI's global approach is the organization, World Doctors Who Respect Human Life. Partially founded by HLI in 1974, this is an alliance of over 300,000 physicians who reject killing of the pre-born.

Armed with the best Pro-Life materials, missionaries in 109 countries distribute HLI information wherever it is needed—from the halls of Congress to school libraries in foreign lands. HLI gives presentations to whoever will listen:

TV and radio audiences, bishops, medical schools, midwives, students, government officials, and others.

HLI's arsenal is a well-stocked bookstore that furnishes everything that a Pro-Lifer would need: books, slides, films, articles, pictures, booklets and fetal development models. Literally tons of these weapons in the Pro-Life battle are shipped free all over the world.

The author has direct experience with HLI's generosity in sharing resources. When I wrote to Fr. Marx requesting information for this publication, I received a *box* of materials. Included were three books and numerous pamphlets and brochures. His best-selling book, *The Death Peddlers: War on the Unborn,* is available in English, Spanish and Japanese. Over 250,000 copies of his booklet, *The Mercy Killers,* have been sold, along with more than 400,000 copies of his pamphlet, *Death Without Dignity.*

His more recent books include *Confessions of a Pro-Life Missionary, Fighting for Life, The Flying Monk* and *Still Fighting for Life.*

Articles by Fr. Paul Marx have appeared in numerous publications in the U.S. and abroad. These include *National Catholic Register, The Wanderer, Marriage and Family* (Canada), *Twin Circle, Homiletic and Pastoral Review, Family* (Italy), *All About Issues, Fidelity, Social Order, Theologisches* (Germany), *Southern Cross* (South Africa) and *Catholic Examiner* (Hong Kong).

The scope of his organization's activities is truly awesome. Rather than detailing all of them, suffice it to say that Fr. Paul Marx and HLI do everything humanly possible to preserve and to promote throughout the world a Pro-Life, pro-God and pro-family way of living. Fr. Marx states, "There is no issue dealing with life or the family that HLI does not handle. And please God, we shall always handle every issue *according* to the mind of the Church."[14]

Fr. Paul Marx, who has devoted his life to combatting the very organized anti-life and anti-family forces worldwide. Fr. Marx has set up branches of his Pro-Life organization, Human Life International, in 52 nations.

9

Brian and Lynn Woznicki

Through modern technology, an amniocentesis can provide the genetic information used to determine the likelihood of birth defects. Combined with the modern quest for the "perfect baby," this technique has contributed greatly to the increase of abortions. In my own sidewalk counseling at the local abortuary, I have myself often heard the argument given that a parent and society are in effect doing an unborn child a favor by killing him or her in the womb if there is a high probability that the baby is deformed or flawed. Integral to this logic is the assumption that life is difficult enough without one's having serious handicaps. How can one really find any joy in living, the reasoning goes, with extra burdens which impede physical or psychological functioning? Favoring birth under these circumstances is depicted as being almost inhumane.

However, concern for the child may not be the real motivation for making the baby in the womb a target for murder. Avoiding inconvenience to parents and to society are more likely reasons for "preventive abortions."

Regardless of the thinking underlying this sort of "mercy killing" in the womb, Pro-Lifers definitely oppose it. Among them are Brian Woznicki and the former Lynn Schnepper, who believe that all human life deserves protection from its very beginning. Their stand is contrary to the "quality-of-life" ethic, which stipulates that expected levels of functioning are a prerequisite to existence.

Brian and Lynn were both born with cerebral palsy. Although Lynn was only mildly affected, Brian's condition is disabling to his motor functions and his speech. However, they both credit their own caring Christian parents with instilling a love of life in them.

The couple met in 1989 through a dating service for the handicapped. Their relationship grew as they revealed more of their lives to each other. One issue important to both of them was their mutual commitment to the sanctity of life. They discovered that they were both Pro-Life activists who had risked arrest in peaceful Rescue efforts. This shared cause became the hallmark of their relationship. These Pro-Lifers were married in June, 1991. They thank God they were not deprived of each other through abortion.

Brian and Lynn Woznicki, both handicapped with cerebral palsy, were drawn together by their mutual commitment to the Pro-Life movement.

10

Cardinal John J. O'Connor

One of the most outspoken Pro-Life religious leaders in America is Cardinal John J. O'Connor of New York. In an era of moral relativism, he is a champion of traditional values based on the teachings of the Roman Catholic Church and Scriptural principles. Fr. Paul Marx of Human Life International declares, "Thanks be to God for the few such as Archbishops O'Connor and Law of New York and Boston, respectively, along with the remnant of our once-solid episcopate."[1] Pro-Life across the board, Cardinal O'Connor confronts the threats of euthanasia and pornography, in addition to abortion.

As one of the most respected spokesmen of the American hierarchy, he was one of the featured speakers at the 1990 Rally for Life in Washington, D. C. He has boldly questioned the media's fairness in reporting Pro-Life events. The Cardinal stirred the crowds to chant, "Tell the truth!"—which was directed at attending newspeople and which eventually emerged as the motto for the rally.

His Eminence has experienced the bias of the media first-hand. He has acknowledged that Church leaders are applauded when they address issues such as hunger and homelessness, but they are discounted when they speak out for life. In addition, he has repeatedly and publicly pledged to help any pregnant woman in New York, free of charge. Although his proclamation dispels the notion that the Catholic Church is more anti-abortion than pro-women, his offer has been consistently ignored by the media.

Cardinal O'Connor was also a special guest speaker at the Unity '90 Video Conference on June 28, 1990. Through a satellite broadcast throughout the nation, he reiterated his commitment to pregnant women. Upholding the fact that every innocent human is entitled to a chance to live, the Cardinal quoted Mother Teresa, who warned that there will be no peace on earth until abortion ends.

Chairman of the U.S. Bishops' Committee for Pro-Life Activities, Cardinal O'Connor released an essay entitled "The Choice Is Life" for Respect Life Month in October, 1990. It expressed his devotion to the cause.

He began this document with the story of Moses, who was "illegally" rescued from the Nile River by the Egyptian princess and her ladies-in-waiting. Because these women chose to disobey the civil law, Moses lived and eventually delivered God's people out of slavery. "No wonder Moses told his people: Choose Life...Only human beings have free will, that is, the freedom to make deliberate choices...We are expected to choose what is reasonable."[2]

Furthermore, Cardinal O'Connor maintains that a reasonable mother would not kill her baby if she were really aware of the implication of her action. "It's simply not natural for a mother to do that."[3]

Encouraged by more objective opinion polls, he is convinced that the nation as a whole will eventually discover that abortion is not natural. Admitting that some disagree with Pro-Lifers about the immorality of abortion, he exhorts love rather than hatred for abortion proponents. This is part of the Christian mandate to love the sinner, but not the sin.

Cardinal O'Connor states that "abortion is the killing of an innocent little human being. About that, science leaves little doubt." He also advocates special compassion for the victim would-be mothers and their parents.

In the document, Cardinal O'Connor restated a part of his column, "Abortion: Questions and Answers" (*Catholic New York,* June 14, 1990):

> The ultimate answer to abortion, I believe, lies in an understanding of love. There is probably no term we use more loosely than love. We often call sexual relations "making love," when no true love may be involved at all. Frequently, we speak of a couple's being "in love," when they are simply experiencing intense infatuation.
>
> Love doesn't come and go with the wind. Love is unselfish, always ready to give. Our Lord tells us that there is no greater love than to lay down our lives for others.
>
> There are good parents who are tempted to encourage a daughter to have an abortion because they love her. Wouldn't it be a wonderful thing if they encouraged her to protect her baby with the same kind of love that they are trying to show toward her? It seems to me that parents must ask themselves if they are thinking of their daughter or of themselves. That question is not intended to be cruel.
>
> Most parents are embarrassed or ashamed if a daughter becomes pregnant outside of wedlock. Abortion can be an all-too-easy way out. In fact, I have known of parents who have virtually forced abortions on daughters who didn't want them. Is that true love?

The Cardinal prescribes abstinence outside of marriage as a way to counteract abortion and to foster mutual respect between the sexes. He opposed the "quick fix" of condom distribution to school children because, among other things, it suggests that children are unable or unwilling to abstain from sexual activity. In other words, His Eminence maintains that "adults must set the standards" for purity and morality. "Adults must be very clear in their own minds that lust is not love."

Furthermore, this Pro-Life leader insists, "Love is always creative, never destructive." Since God has blessed human beings by allowing them to share in His creative process, this process should not be abused in any way. In addition to the pre-born, he also admonishes us to embrace the lives of the disabled, the blind, the deaf and the retarded.

Aware of the frustrations and disappointments Pro-Lifers continually face, he encourages them with these uplifting words:

> Finally, only God knows what Pro-Life workers have accomplished; how many lives they may have saved, how many men and women they have helped, how many families. But of this we can be absolutely certain: without such efforts, the Pro-Life movement would have long since died...Thank God for them.[4]

More recently, on June 13, 1992, Cardinal O'Connor joined a massive Pro-Life prayer vigil through Manhattan. The event began with Mass and ended with prayer outside an abortuary.

Cardinal John J. O'Connor, one of the most outspoken Pro-Life religious leaders in America in an era of moral cowardice among many Churchmen. Cardinal O'Connor points out that Moses was "illegally" rescued from death—and lived to fulfill a great mission from God.

11

Randall Terry

Because more than 26 million pre-born babies have been sacrificed in the United States to the modern gods of convenience, pleasure and personal reputation since the 1973 Roe v. Wade decision, Randall Terry has stepped forward in their defense and has become one of the most prominent leaders in the Pro-Life movement.

Randall Terry founded the organization called "Operation Rescue." Those who do "Rescue" work sit in front of abortuary entrances in an attempt to deny access to pregnant women planning to kill their babies. This intervention may give sidewalk counselors an opportunity to provide these women with the truth about abortion and with options for life, such as referrals to crisis pregnancy centers. Rescues are conducted peacefully and in a spirit of personal sacrifice. Rescuers must agree to an honorable code of conduct before participating. As part of an effort to impede the killing process, they are instructed to become limp when confronted with arrest, in order to force police to resort to removing them physically.

Operation Rescue is Scripturally based on *Proverbs* 24:11: "Rescue those who are unjustly sentenced to death; don't stand back and let them die."[1]

Randall Terry began his Pro-Life work as a picketer and by founding programs for women—which included a crisis pregnancy center in 1984 and a home for unwed mothers in 1986. However, he "began to wrestle with our responsibility to obey God's word above and beyond our obedience to man's laws."[2] Consequently, he helped organize the first official "Operation Rescue" mission in January, 1986. Since that time, Operation Rescue has spread to various cities throughout the nation, with Randall Terry providing leadership and inspiration to local Rescue organizations. To date, over 40,000 Rescuers have been arrested and it has been confirmed that hundreds of babies have been saved.[3]

Randall Terry was a leader of the 1991 "Summer of Mercy" series of Rescues in Wichita, Kansas. This was organized in the town where George Tiller performs third-trimester abortions. More than 2,000 persons were arrested in this effort to save the pre-born, which brought national attention.

Pro-Lifers have suffered many atrocities nationwide because of police brutality aimed at breaking up and discouraging Rescues. A stark example is a 1989 Pittsburgh Rescue in which female Pro-Lifers complained of being demeaned by physical abuse and even sexual molestation.[4]

City police departments that have "distinguished" themselves by "torture-type" techniques include Los Angeles (where excruciating pain-compliance techniques were used on Rescuers),[5] West Hartford, Connecticut (where bones were broken)[6] and San Diego (where police employed nunchakus, which are a martial arts device).[7]

Randall Terry has himself courageously endured much suffering and persecution for saving babies. With 35 arrests in nine cities, he has spent over 7 months in jail.[8] This includes 4 months in a prison work camp,[9] where he was incarcerated with dangerous felons.[10] The courts were obviously attempting to punish him for his leadership role in Rescue operations by imposing on him a harsh sentence for a misdemeanor offense.

Like the prophets of the Old Testament, Randall Terry is

a voice for traditional Judeo-Christian values. He warns, "We are at war for the soul of our nation and the future of our children."[11] Schools are one of the critical battlegrounds in this war, according to Mr. Terry. As an example, he cites immoral sex education programs (which teach promiscuity) as outrageous intrusions into our school environments and as attempts to pervert our children. Furthermore, this Pro-Life leader condemns school-based clinics, which distribute birth control devices and promote abortions.

He identifies Planned Parenthood, the "nation's single largest abortion provider,"[12] as the organization behind this effort to corrupt our school children. "Planned Parenthood is not only determined to devalue and destroy your children; they are also determined to do it with or without your permission. Their attitude is simple: If you parents don't like us giving birth control and abortions to your children, to hell with you."[13]

Randall Terry believes that even Christians often reflect an anti-family attitude in their views about children. Instead of extolling children as a blessing, as exemplified in *Psalm* 127[126]:3-5, many so-called believers feel negative about having larger families. Randall Terry calls upon Christians to repent of and abandon this attitude.

Because of the abuse received by Rescuers and because of governmental oppression of Christian values in general, Randall Terry warns that our constitutional rights and our religious liberties are in danger. To meet this threat, he founded the Christian Defense Coalition in April, 1990 "to train Christians to defend each other from police brutality, judicial tyranny and political harassment."[14]

In a further effort to protect Rescuers from abuse, Randall Terry has organized a more recent program, the American Anti-Persecution League (AAPL). Lawyers funded by the League will sue those who violate the rights of Pro-Lifers. "Brutal police, homosexual thugs, savage radical feminists and cold-blooded abortion-mill guards"[15] will be among those whom AAPL attorneys intend to confront for physically harming Pro-Lifers. AAPL will provide equal protection under the law to Rescuers and thereby help them to continue to save babies. Donations may be made to AAPL, Attn.: Randall Terry, 504 S. Beach Blvd., Suite 426, Anaheim, CA 92804.

Randall Terry believes that Christians will be "given over" to anti-life evils if they continue to tolerate them through their inaction. He calls upon Christians to take the initiative by promoting Christian principles, and he encourages believers to run for political office in order to effect change. He cites the need for "God-fearing statesmen," rather than "cowardly politicians."[16]

His writings, which are eloquent and straightforwardly expressed, include his two books, *Operation Rescue* (Whitaker House) and *Accessory to Murder* (Wolgemuth & Hyatt, Publishers, Inc.); the latter was written from a prison work camp. He has also produced an Operation Rescue video, which is available from Operation Rescue.

In addition to *Focus on the Family,* Randall Terry has appeared on ABC's *Nightline,* CBN's *The 700 Club, Straight Talk, The Oprah Winfrey Show, The Morton Downey Jr. Show* and CNN's *Crossfire.* In addition, *20/20, 48 Hours* and PBS have featured him in documentaries. Randall Terry is obviously an important voice for the many future little citizens who cannot yet speak for themselves.

As with many personages in the Scriptures who were called by God to do some special work, Randall Terry is relatively young—only 32 years old as of this writing. He is married, and he and his wife Cindy are the parents of one child and have 3 foster children. Randall Terry is a graduate of Elim Bible Institute in Lima, New York.

Randall Terry may be contacted at P.O. Box 2002, Binghamton, NY 13902.

Randall Terry, founder in 1986 of Operation Rescue. Rescues are non-violent direct interventions in which Pro-Lifers sit in front of abortion clinic entrances in order to deny access to pregnant women. To date over 40,000 Rescuers have been arrested and hundreds of babies have been confirmed saved.

12
Woody Jenkins

The evening of July 6, 1990 was an historic moment in the Louisiana legislature. Representative Louis "Woody" Jenkins was spearheading the most protective legislation on behalf of pre-born children in the history of this nation. Louisiana's Governor had already vetoed the anti-abortion measure because it did not provide exceptions for rape and incest. Overriding a governor's veto has never occurred in Louisiana in this century, rendering it a near impossibility. However, Representative Jenkins is a man of deep faith and believes that, with God, anything is possible.

That evening was the culmination of much preparation. A month earlier, the legislature's House Committee on Criminal Justice had convened to consider the abortion issue. Eight out of ten of its members had already publicly declared that they would not support an anti-abortion bill which did not include exceptions for rape and incest.

State Representative Jenkins led the campaign to win this committee over to a "pure" Pro-Life position, which would not include these exceptions. With the assistance of Americans United for Life, he brought in expert witnesses of the highest caliber.

One of the world's foremost geneticists, Dr. Jerome Lejeune from Paris, awed the committee with compelling testimony on the beginnings of human life. He told how the DNA of the male unites with the DNA of the female, with their accompanying twenty-three chromosomes, to form a completely separate being at the very moment of conception. He elaborated on the fact that the multitude of individual characteristics of each human being are determined at that instant. These range from physical attributes, such as the color of hair or the color of eyes, to personal talents, such as musical abilities.

Committee members marvelled at Dr. Lejeune's description of the DNA molecule itself. Although it is only one millimeter long (.039 of an inch) and wound very minutely, it can store enough information to fill five complete sets of *The Encyclopedia Britannica.*

Dr. Lejeune cited the recent discoveries of the Englishman Jeffrey, who found that the DNA molecule stores information in the smallest possible way in a configuration similar to the bar codes on items in a grocery store.

This famous geneticist ended his testimony with the inescapable conclusion that all people are indeed human from the moment of conception and that our fundamentally unique nature as individuals remains the same after that time.

Next Dr. Jerome Gasser, a renowned embryologist at the Louisiana State University Medical School, explained the intricacies of cellular development. Committee members were informed that "the human being is never an undifferentiated mass of protoplasm, or blob. There is always specialization."[1] Furthermore, the first cell is the most complex in human growth. From the moment of conception, the sex, hair color, propensity for athletics, and a thousand other traits are determined. From the moment of conception onward there exists a new human being—a man or a woman, rather than an "it."

Other distinguished physicians described the need to care for pre-born children as separate patients. A former abortion-clinic manager shared her experiences, telling how she finally realized that she was killing babies while she was cleaning up dismembered body parts after abortions at the clinic where she worked.

After two days of unprecedented testimony about the beginning of human life, the committee voted unanimously for a bill against abortion that contained no exceptions. They "came to realize that the little baby didn't bring himself or herself into existence. Whether conceived in rape or incest or by mistake or whatever it was, this child is a human being."[2]

Furthermore, Woody Jenkins' committee discovered that Louisiana law, since 1825, has recognized the personhood of the pre-born from conception onward. These legislators questioned how the U.S. Supreme Court could contradict this fact: Either a pre-born is a person, or he or she is not—no middle ground is possible.

Although all committee members were finally convinced of the humanity of the pre-born, they knew that this biological fact would still be pitted against the burning issue of rape in the Louisiana Legislature.

Ironically, Roe v. Wade was based on a phony rape case; Jane Roe (Norma McCorvey) publicly admitted in 1987 that she had not been raped at all.[3] Twenty-six million abortion-murders have resulted from a lie that went all the way to the Supreme Court and changed "the law of the land."

Woody Jenkins also knew that rape was not a significant factor in Louisiana abortions. A typical year (1987) revealed just one case of either rape or incest out of 15,700 reported abortions![4]

Jenkins realized that allowing exceptions would make Louisiana's law self-contradictory and give it no chance to be upheld by the courts.

> We cannot argue on the one hand that the unborn child is a legal person and entitled to the protection of the 14th Amendment, which says no one should

be deprived of life. . .without due process of law, and
then say that it is legal to kill some of these unborn
persons without due process. In the companion case
to Roe v. Wade, Doe v. Bolton, the Supreme Court
made it clear that a state must be consistent. Either
the unborn is a person or he isn't.[5]

Representative Jenkins believed that even if such a law were
upheld, thousands of women would, like Jane Roe, falsely
allege rape as an excuse to justify abortion. He asserted, "I
can tell you this, the person who is of a mind to kill her
unborn child may have no problem about lying about the
nature of the conception."[6]

Woody Jenkins stood firm on the fact that human life
begins at conception and that every person deserves protection, regardless of his or her beginning. Concerning abortion,
he declared, "It is the murder of children, and there can be
no compromise with it."[7]

Consequently, he prayed and called on the assistance of
Almighty God in the July 6, 1990 battle in the Louisiana
House on the issue of abortion. His forces realized that they
were at least six votes short of the two-thirds majority
required for a veto override. Intense pressure on undecided
Representatives yielded only four more possible votes. With
the fate of the bill remaining in serious jeopardy, Woody
Jenkins' hopes began to falter.

However, at a critical moment, an ally walked into the
chambers. He was Representative Bernard Carrier. Although
Dr. Carrier had been sick at home 35 miles from Baton
Rouge, the Jenkins camp had summoned him in their hour
of need.

Dr. Carrier made his entrance just before the voting, leading most members of the House to believe that his sudden
presence was part of a well-formed plan to override the veto.
They concluded that the Jenkins group must have enough
votes to accomplish their objective. Apparently as the result

of the intervention of Divine Providence, other uncommitted lawmakers voted in favor of the override in order to be on the winning side. The override passed in the House.

The next day brought the battle to the Louisiana Senate, where the President of the Senate was opposed to the override. Anticipating massive citizen support for it, he had ordered the state police to lock the doors of the capitol building. This was unprecedented in Louisiana history. With daytime temperatures outside in the 90's, the President of the Senate finally allowed about 200 people to enter. However, he ordered that no communication could transpire between the legislators and the observers. According to Woody Jenkins, "The plan was to totally isolate the members of the Senate from the people of our state so that they couldn't be influenced."[8]

However, over 10,000 Pro-Lifers gathered outside the Senate chambers, chanting: "Override! Override! Override! Override!"[9] Their voices could be heard blaring through the four-foot thick granite walls of the chambers during the six hours of the Senate debate. Although the temperature reached 95 degrees that day, the refrain grew louder. People of every denomination fervently prayed in their own unique styles in the midst of the chanting.

Woody Jenkins was moved to the depths of his being by this awesome demonstration of love for the pre-born. He concluded, "I knew at that time that regardless of the outcome of the Senate vote, it really didn't matter. We had won the Pro-Life argument in Louisiana. And Louisiana was then, and will always be, a Pro-Life state."[10]

Pro-Lifers lost the override in the Senate by just three votes on that sweltering July day, but Woody Jenkins and his fellow lawmakers resumed the battle again in 1991. The Louisiana Legislature over-rode the Governor's veto to pass HB112. Although this legislation allows exceptions for rape and incest, it provides a direct challenge to Roe v. Wade. In the meantime, Woody Jenkins will continue to work for a no-exceptions anti-abortion law.

This Louisiana legislator is not an ordinary politician—he is a statesman. Rather than voting on political expediency, he decides on moral principle.

A man of great courage, Woody Jenkins proclaims, "Our job is not to reflect opinion polls. Our job is to fashion opinion...You can't say that life begins at conception, and then say some people can be killed without due process."[11]

In the face of almost overwhelming opposition, he is not going to retreat from the fact that human life begins at conception. Furthermore, he exhorts his colleagues to join him in this battle with the following inspiring and encouraging statement:

> I want to challenge you to go forth from this day, to use your special commission to save the lives of these unborn children and change the world. I pray that God will give us the wisdom and the courage to know what to do and how to do it.[12]

Finally, Representative Jenkins alerts Pro-Life forces that they are not simply fighting human pro-abortion forces. He identifies the real enemy in this battle:

> If you want to find out who we are fighting, you look at *Ephesians* 6:12: "We wrestle not against flesh and blood, but against principalities, against powers, against the rulers of the darkness of this world, against spiritual wickedness in high places." That is where we are fighting.[13]

*   *   *

It has just been reported that on September 22, 1992 a U.S. Appellate Court overturned the Louisiana pro-life law. Further developments are awaited.

Representative Louis "Woody" Jenkins and his family. Representative Jenkins led the dramatic campaign to override the Louisiana Governor's veto of a no-exceptions Pro-Life bill in July of 1990. During the 6-hour Senate debate, over 10,000 Pro-Life Louisianans gathered outside the chambers in 95° heat to pray and to chant their support for the pre-born.

13

Don Brady

As Judeo-Christian values have become weaker in our present society, our news media has generally grown more secularized. This bias is blatant in the case of the abortion issue, which is framed as a "reproductive choice" or "right to privacy" dispute. The major TV networks and newspapers betray their slant by their terminology. For example, a ruling overturning Roe v. Wade would "take away a woman's Constitutional right to have an abortion," according to a popular broadcaster, almost as if abortion on demand were written into the U.S. Constitution.

Information not even mentioned by the media is also of great significance. Biological facts on fetal development or graphic photos of aborted babies are conspicuous by their absence in the news. Instead, situations casting abortion in a favorable light are showcased. Stories directed at the evils of "teen-age pregnancy" are commonly illustrated, with abortion presumed to be the obvious solution.

This "pro-choice" (i.e., pro-abortion) mentality has been subconsciously accepted by many in our society whose thinking is largely shaped by the media, especially by TV. For a newsperson to counter this trend requires the courage to support life in what has become almost a death culture. But Don Brady at the *Rockford Labor News* in Rockford, Illinois is a publisher who exemplifies this fortitude.

Other than *The Observer,* the official Catholic newspaper in the Rockford diocese, the weekly *Labor News* is the only area publication known to the author of this book which takes a strong Pro-Life position. Since the local death mill's anticipated move in 1985 to its present location at 1400 Broadway—next door to the *Labor News,* in an old school building—Don Brady has frequently dedicated space on his front page to attacking the evil of abortion. "A Broadway Butchery? No!,"[1] "East Side Awaits First Execution of Unborn Babies,"[2] and "Profit in Abortion? You Figure It Out"[3] are three headlines that boldly forewarned readers about the reality of abortion.

However, almost immediately after the 1973 Roe v. Wade decision legalizing abortion, the *Labor News* had alerted the community to the existence of a local slaughterhouse for pre-born children. "Where Women May Order the Extermination of Unborn"[4] was the March 16, 1973 headline, with an arrow pointing to a photo of the building where Dr. Richard Ragsdale, the local abortionist, had begun his grizzly trade.

In addition to keeping the issue in the forefront of the community's consciousness by citing the evil of abortion, the paper reports on Pro-Life activities around the area. Its building also provides Pro-Life activists with an easily accessible place to store picket signs and is a haven for Pro-Lifers who seek warmth during cold weather.

Don Brady is a faithful Catholic, who receives Communion on a daily basis. By sacrificing some of his business to save the pre-born, he is storing up treasures in Heaven. His courage provides an example for those committed to the truth.

Don Brady, publisher of the *Rockford Labor News*, a local newspaper which openly supports the pre-born and attacks abortion. Don Brady also provides support to Pro-Life witnesses at the local abortuary, which is located next door to the *Labor News* office.

14

Doctor John C. Willke

The term "doctor" usually evokes benevolent images in our minds. We may recall childhood experiences in which parents took us to this special professional person in order to help us get well. Although we sometimes feared the sting of an injection on our tender behinds, we trusted that it was for our well-being. The classic Norman Rockwell paintings, "Doctor's Office" and "Doctor and Doll," are affectionate caricatures of these mostly fond remembrances.

For some people, the word "doctor" may be associated with critical assistance in emergency situations, ranging from the joys of childbirth to the trauma of accidents. Doctors also perform important major surgeries or compassionately help the terminally ill to accept death.

Whatever the situation, physicians have been traditionally perceived as the dominant figure in health care—those most knowledgeable and most capable of helping us, those who have their patients' best interests in mind. Physicians are people whom we literally trust with our lives.

However, certain doctors have shattered the positive image of their profession. Instead of healers motivated to foster life, they have become destroyers of life. Some Nazi physicians were examples of this. Participating in grizzly and inhumane experiments on their victims, these twisted individuals shocked mankind with their cruelty and callousness. In our own times, abortion practitioners have acted contrary to the Hippocratic tradition by providing abortions, even on demand. Using a variety of methods, they have routinely killed pre-born infants. While usually citing humanitarian motives for their trade, they are suspected and accused by Pro-Lifers of having money as their prime objective.

Although some doctors have thus prostituted themselves, many others have remained faithful to their profession of fostering human health and well-being and have fought for the rights of the pre-born. Among these honorable men, one particularly distinguishes himself, John C. Willke, M.D. Dr. Willke is internationally respected as a long-time champion of babies in the womb. From the depth of his heart, Dr. Willke states, "I believe that abortion is the cutting edge of the greatest evil of our time. When and if we can turn back this evil tide, then I believe many other values will fall back in place."[1]

Having outstanding qualifications and credentials, Dr. Willke is no light-weight. A Diplomat and Fellow of the American Board of Family Practice, he was a practicing physician in Cincinnati, Ohio for 40 years. This Pro-Life advocate is an accredited supervisor of Family Life Education and is qualified as a counselor.

A founding life member of the National Alliance for Family Life, he was also on the senior attending staff of the Providence and Good Samaritan Hospitals in Cincinnati. Dr. Willke is the president of the International Right-to-Life Federation and was a founding board member of that organization in 1973. He was formerly president of the National Right-to-Life Committee (NRLC), which includes 50 state and almost 3,000 local chapters. This organization issues an official newspaper, which for some time was published by Dr. Willke.

His daily radio program, *Life Issues with Dr. John C. Willke,* is aired on over 365 stations. A respected spokesman for the Pro-Life movement, Dr. Willke is available at his Life

Issues Institute headquarters office in Cincinnati. Dr. Willke is the founding president of the Institute. The Institute collects and catalogs Pro-Life educational materials for distribution. Dedicated to serving the needs of the Pro-Life movement, it also refers individuals and groups to appropriate information and speakers.

Highly regarded by the media, Dr. Willke averages about 1,000 radio and TV appearances each year. Examples include the following broadcasts: *The Phil Donahue Show, 60 Minutes, Good Morning America, The Today Show,* ABC's *Nightline, The MacNeil/Lehrer Report, Crossfire, Focus on the Family, The 700 Club* and *Geraldo,* plus other appearances on NBC and CBS News and C-SPAN. In addition, *People Magazine* and the *Washington Post Magazine* have featured Dr. Willke.

Dr. Willke is one of the most acclaimed physician authors in the Right-to-Life field. His classic, *Handbook on Abortion,* was the most widely read book in the world on abortion and scientifically pleads the case for the pre-born. The first edition was published in 1971, pre-dating the 1973 Roe v. Wade decision. Having spoken out before abortion even became legalized, Dr. Willke is a true pioneer in the Pro-Life crusade. In *Handbook on Abortion,* the Willkes' goal was to set forth the scientific, medical and social reasons against abortion. Among the many topics covered in this extremely informative book were the beginning of life (with the fertilized ovum), how abortions are done, maternal deaths from legal abortion, harm to the mother's health, the "population explosion," fetal experimentation, abortion after rape or incest, mental health during pregnancy, euthanasia, and our ageing population. The *Handbook on Abortion* has been recently replaced with the book, *Abortion Questions and Answers* (which is also available in video and slide form). This book is certain to be another milestone in Pro-Life literature.

Dr. Willke and his wife, Barbara, who is also a doctor,

are co-authors of 10 books on abortion and human sexuality and are contributing authors to four others. Seven of their audio-visual works and a variety of handy brochures have also been published. Their writings have been translated into 19 languages, and they have included articles in over 70 publications.

With a primary concern for the pre-born and the would-be-mother victims, Dr. Willke's materials are reasonably priced to facilitate the widest possible readership.

This author was privileged to hear Dr. Willke personally at the Rally for Life in Washington in April, 1990. Featured as one of the main speakers, he inspired the huge crowd gathered at the Washington Monument to persevere in the battle to save the pre-born. John Cardinal O'Connor, Vice President Dan Quayle and Dr. James Dobson were among the other notables personally encouraging those present. Hailed as the biggest gathering in the 200-year history of the nation's capital, the Rally for Life assembled hundreds of thousands of Pro-Lifers to stand up for the pre-born.

Partners in marriage and in the Pro-Life movement, Dr. Willke and his wife, Barbara, have 6 children and 13 grandchildren. Their relationship is a tribute to traditional family values and is a Christian witness for life.

John C. Willke, M.D., who may well be the most famous Pro-Life spokesman in the world. Along with his wife, Dr. Willke authored the world-famous *Handbook on Abortion*, which was published as early as 1971—as well as many other books and publications. Dr. Willke frequently appears on national radio and TV broadcasts.

15

Joe Scheidler

Born into a devoutly religious family, Joe Scheidler learned at an early age that abortion is a grave sin—so grave in the eyes of the Roman Catholic Church that it carried with it the ban of excommunication. After high school and a stint in the Navy, he entered Notre Dame University and received a degree in journalism. Joe worked as a reporter for one year and then entered the seminary for eight years. During this time, he dedicated himself to the study of morality, which included that of abortion. Not having a vocation to the priesthood, he left the seminary in 1959 with a profound, deeply studied view of morality, which included an absolute conviction that abortion is indeed murder.[1]

Joe returned to his alma mater as a professor and later taught in a Chicago-area college. He married a former student, Ann Crawley, in 1965. By the time the 1973 Roe v. Wade decision legalized child-killing, Ann was pregnant with their fourth child. At the time, Joe was working in the field of public relations, but he was shocked by the Supreme Court ruling. Joe decided almost immediately to fight it. A few months later he organized the Chicago office for Pro-Life Publicity to convince the public of the gross injustice of this decision. Since that time, he has dedicated his entire life to preventing abortion.[2]

Honored by Presidential candidate Patrick Buchanan as the "Green Beret of the Pro-Life Movement,"[3] Joe is the Executive Director of the Pro-Life Action League in Chicago. Nonviolent direct action is the hallmark of the League, which attacks abortion on numerous fronts and is responsible for saving thousands of lives. In Chicago alone, eight abortion clinics have been closed through sidewalk counseling, picketing and Rescue missions. Recruitment and training provided by the League to Pro-Life organizations nationwide have resulted in nearly a hundred abortuaries shutting their doors.[4]

However, this organization's activism goes beyond confrontations at abortion mills and includes facing up to pro-abortion politicians and pro-abortion organizations like the National Organization of Women (NOW) and Planned Parenthood,[5] the latter of which is the largest abortion promoter in the country.[6] The Pro-Life Action League fights all those who support abortion: the doctors, the judges, the clinics, the drug companies, the phony "charities," the liberal media, the politicians, the corporations that contribute to abortion, and even the pro-abortion wing among churches.[7] Deeply concerned for pregnant women, the League also has a close relationship with problem pregnancy centers.[8]

Joe Scheidler states that the woman involved in an abortion can be an innocent victim, just like the baby. He has witnessed young women being physically coerced into entering an abortion clinic. One was dragged in by her scarf; another was escorted into the building in a hammerlock.

When the author requested a statement from Joe Scheidler for this book, the following was his response. It reflects Mr. Scheidler's firm resolve to rid the nation of the abomination of abortion and it identifies his various strategies in this battle:

> My involvement in the activist Pro-Life movement
> is based on the equation that abortion equals murder.
> It will make sense only to those who believe without
> question that abortion is the unjust, premeditated

taking of innocent human life.

In America, a violent death from abortion takes place every twenty seconds. That is a total of 4,500 deaths every day, 1.7 million abortions each year. Slaughter of a nation's posterity will destroy that nation, both physically and spiritually. America is being destroyed by the killing of its children before they are born.

Those who understand abortion and want to stop it have an obligation to recruit others into the Pro-Life movement and to pass on to them their experience and expertise, so that in time, the injustice of abortion will end. Pro-Life activists cannot wait for the legislative and judicial process that will make abortion illegal. The activist has to save lives now.

No social movement in the history of this country has succeeded without activists taking to the streets. Activism, including demonstrations, pickets, protest and rescues, is necessary, not only to save lives, but to garner public attention, to bring the media into the struggle, and to shake politicians into recognizing the determination of anti-abortion supporters. Anyone who misses this purpose of activism is a poor student of history.

It is not enough to believe in the value of life and to condemn abortion. We must act on our conviction that every unborn human life is of inestimable value, of itself, to society and in the eyes of God.

My commitment is based on an act of faith. I take the belief in defenseless human life seriously and propose to save those lives through suffering, sacrifice, prayer and action. I am responding to the Lord's command to go and teach. My methods often result in complaints filed with the police and in lawsuits filed in the courts, but they also result in birth certificates filed for children who were scheduled for execution.

As long as I can save a life, I will be a Pro-Life activist.[9]

Joe Scheidler is obviously a man who translates his faith boldly into action, regardless of the cost to himself. "So faith also, if it have not works, is dead in itself." (*James* 2:17). Totally committed to the Pro-Life cause, Joe also attacks the evils associated with abortion, such as school-based clinics (which pass out contraceptives to school students) and fetal experimentation.

The author has personally heard Joe Scheidler address Pro-Life gatherings. A dynamic speaker, Joe condemns abortion as the worst evil. He compares abortion to the killing of children in concentration camps in World War II. Invoking Scripture passages which prescribe deferential treatment for children, he warns that our treatment of them will enter into our Final Judgment by God.

The truest test of a Christian, he maintains, is whether he or she loves the innocent. "The baby in the womb is our business because he is one of God's little ones," he asserts. "We need to fight abortion with all our might!"

Joe Scheidler admonishes his audiences that Pro-Lifers are to follow God's law rather than man's law regarding trespass statutes. He compares Rescuers who enter private property to save the pre-born to those heroes who would jump a fence with a "No Trespass" sign on it to save a child drowning in a pool. To support this type of action Scripturally, he cites *Proverbs* 24:11, which states: "Deliver them that are led to death: and those that are drawn to death forbear not to deliver." (See the Randall Terry profile for more information on Rescues.)

Challenging the Supreme Court's 1973 Roe v. Wade decision, he charges that there is nothing in our Constitution which justifies abortion.

This Chicagoan claims that abortion is the act closest to "God-killing," since it serves to destroy God's plan in nature.

Urging others to be more committed to the cause of the pre-born, he likens fighting unselfishly for life with sainthood. He insists that many lives have been saved by the Pro-Life movement, making its actions eminently worthwhile.

However, Joe Scheidler also assures his audiences that Pro-Lifers will suffer on the road to sanctity for their commitment to the pre-born. That suffering, he says, could include incurring public scorn and abuse, loss of jobs, physical harm, and possible arrest and imprisonment. Of course, Our Lord promised us persecution: "If the world hate you, know ye, that it hath hated me before you." (*John* 15:18). Joe also recalls his own arrest during an anti-abortion demonstration in the company of a top religious leader in New York.

Joe Scheidler advises Pro-Lifers to continue to pressure for a change in laws and to persist in sidewalk counseling at abortion mills. He encourages Pro-Lifers with his optimistic report of the numerous abortion clinics closed nationwide due to the Pro-Life movement.

The Pro-Life Action League also keeps media attention focused on abortion through the promotion of publicity. Stimulating and provocative, Joe Scheidler is sought as a guest on radio and TV shows. These have included ABC's *News Nightline, The Phil Donahue Show, Crossfire, Face the Nation, Good Morning America, The MacNeil/Lehrer Report* and others.

Joe Scheidler has written a book on his methods of fighting abortion, entitled *CLOSED: 99 Ways to Stop Abortion.* His video, *Meet the Abortion Providers,* features former abortionists who are now telling the truth about this grizzly trade.

The Pro-Life Action League publishes a quarterly newsletter, *Pro-Life Action News,* to update members on the latest developments, successes and current projects. Joe Scheidler's office maintains an extensive Pro-Life library to provide information for reporters, legislators and educators. The League conducts a 24-hour news hotline, with a new message three times a week. The phone number is 312-777-2525.

Joe Scheidler, founder of the Chicago-based Pro-Life Action League, who has been called "the Green Beret of the Pro-Life movement." Through the League's efforts, eight abortion clinics have been shut down in Chicago alone, and through its training of other Pro-Lifers almost 100 abortion clinics have been shut down nationwide—thus saving thousands of lives.

16

Mary Cunningham Agee

The 1973 Roe v. Wade decision legalized abortion in the United States. Since that ruling, women have been able to exercise a "choice" to terminate their pregnancies. However, the founder of a unique program maintains that many women are not really given a "choice," but are cajoled into aborting because of a perceived absence of practical alternatives in giving life to their babies. Mary Cunningham Agee's mission is to provide such realistic alternatives to abortion through her "Nurturing Network."

Mary's sincere concern for pregnant women began after she suffered a miscarriage in 1984. Although she experienced tremendous grief, she overcame her loss and later worked through her own emotions so that she can now truly empathize with others enduring similar losses, including women with post-abortion depression.

Mary was determined to investigate the problems peculiar to women with crisis pregnancies before taking any specific action. The results of a survey she conducted among these women were surprising. More than 90% of the women "choosing" abortion would have "preferred to find a positive alternative"[1] if they had been offered a practical way to follow their heart.

Although Mary's study was informal and based on a rela-

tively small sample (with about 100 women responding), it
provided her with valuable insight into a little-explored
problem area. Mary saw a great need to help women "remove
the crisis, not the pregnancy." This conclusion became a
motto for The Nurturing Network, a motto which The Network continually puts into practice in a warm and loving way
by offering practical help to pregnant women at this very vulnerable time in their lives.

The Nurturing Network has served over 3,600 clients since
it began its work in 1985. In addition, the "Network" has
the support of 12,500 members, who are located in all 50
states. These are people and organizations who are committed
to helping pregnant women make a choice for life, rather than
for abortion. They include people in such fields as social
work, counseling, education and medicine, as well as
employers, foster families and individual friends of the
organization.

A typical client case will illustrate how the program works:
Sue is a 25-year-old graduate student who has a semester left
to go to earn her advanced degree. Completing her degree
will mean a substantial pay difference for her on the job. She
meets a young man on campus whom she falls in love with.
Sue does not consider herself a "loose" woman, but she
occasionally engages in sex with someone if she feels
strongly enough about him.

Because her romances never previously resulted in pregnancy, Sue is confident that it will not occur from her present
affair. However, this time it is different.

And to her disappointment, her boyfriend is not ready to
take the responsibility for his part in the conception. In addition, the college is a religious institution, which frowns on
unwed pregnancies.

Sue fears her friends will further compound her dilemma
by making embarrassing comments to her, such as, "You
should have known better."

Phoning The Nurturing Network headquarters in Boise,

Idaho puts Sue in contact with Mrs. Agee or one of the 10 Network staff members. Sue is offered immediate support to help stabilize her emotionally in her crisis. Next, her needs are assessed and a plan is developed to help her carry her child to term.

Mercy and compassion are the hallmarks of the planning process. For Mary, reaching out to women through The Nurturing Network is more than a mere profession. It is an expression of her deep faith in God and her love for pregnant women in need and their unborn children. She declares that the key to her mission is, "Take care of the woman and she'll take care of the child."

In Sue's case, The Network is able to arrange admission to and financial aid at an out-of-state college with courses that are comparable to those Sue is presently taking—but the dormitories are full. However, The Nurturing Network knows of a family in a nearby town that is willing to provide a caring home for her during the remainder of her pregnancy.

The Nurturing Network also assists Sue in obtaining prenatal care and helps her find a social service agency for adoption counseling or parenting classes if she feels this would be helpful to her in making the best choice for her and her baby. The Network also helps Sue schedule interviews with employers who do not stigmatize unwed mothers.

The Nurturing Network never coerces or moralizes with its clients. Its mission is to provide practical alternatives to abortion so that a woman can "choose life" for her unborn child without sacrificing her own future plans.

Our typical case depiction shows that The Nurturing Network is an organization providing *comprehensive* assistance. It is dedicated to the total needs of women in crisis pregnancies, be those needs medical, financial, educational or emotional—or involving adoption, parenthood, housing or career. The Network provides a way for women to receive help from individuals, families, agencies, companies, congregations and foundations.

Although it serves anyone in need by networking with social service agencies and crisis pregnancy centers across the country, The Network specializes in meeting the needs of college and working women ages 20-35, for whom the least help is available. According to Mary Agee, these women generally feel very alone, and they face tremendous pressure from family, friends and colleagues to have an abortion.

The available services in most communities are designed to meet the needs of younger women. Mary Agee believes that society offers little understanding to the single working woman who becomes pregnant. Her focus at The Nurturing Network is to provide practical assistance when a woman's family, friends and colleagues have failed to offer the support she so desperately needs.

A former business executive who earned her Master's degree from The Harvard Business School, Mary Agee has credentials that are indeed impressive. She now utilizes her business and interpersonal skills as the volunteer Executive Director of the not-for-profit Nurturing Network.

Mary Agee and The Nurturing Network have received an increasing amount of media coverage, in publications ranging from *Reader's Digest* and *The Wall Street Journal* to *Our Sunday Visitor* and *Liguorian*. Mary Agee received acknowledgment from both sides of the abortion debate when she explained her program on the *ABC News* Special, "Abortion—The New Civil War," which was narrated by Peter Jennings in the Fall of 1990.

Mary has made other appearances on CBS *This Morning, The Christopher Close-Up,* CBS *News Nightwatch,* and the *Hour Magazine Show.* Most recently, she shared her experiences on Dr. James Dobson's *Focus on the Family* radio program. Mary Agee has been nominated for and has received many distinguished awards and honors. She is on the board of numerous organizations.

Through The Nurturing Network Mary Agee has transformed her own hurt and pain into an outreach of hope and practical help for others in need. She believes deeply that God asks each of us to "convert the stones of judgment and apathy into the bread of compassion," and this is the aim of her work.

The Nurturing Network can be contacted by writing to 910 Main Street, Suite 360, P.O. Box 2050, Boise, ID 83701 or by phoning Toll-Free, 1-800-TNN-4MOM. All services provided by The Network are free and confidential. The Nurturing Network welcomes new members and also welcomes financial contributions to help carry on its valuable work.

Mary Cunningham Agee, founder and director of The Nurturing Network, which provides compassionate, practical assistance to help pregnant women choose life for their babies. Mary's aim is to "remove the crisis, not the pregnancy." The Network has served over 3,600 clients since it began in 1985.

17

Attorney Cyrus Zal

If a person enters a burning building to rescue inhabitants, this courageous individual need not be concerned about any trespass law. Even if the property is posted with "No Trespassing" signs, our courts recognize the "necessity defense," which means that this law is superseded by a greater good—saving a human life.

This defense applies to any conceivable situation involving a victim at risk, except one—murder by abortion.[1] In undying loyalty to a death decision, most judges adhere to the 1973 Roe v. Wade ruling, legalizing abortion. Those involved in Operation Rescue are almost always tried on charges such as trespassing, without regard to their motives for crossing property lines.

By courts' adhering strictly to the Roe v. Wade decision, trial proceedings are greatly facilitated. Prosecutors need only prove the technical charges against the defendant, and judges then rule on them only. In trying those who engage in Operation Rescue, *the judicial system is not "bothered" by the colossal life-and-death issue of child-killing,* which actually lies at the base of all these court cases.

If you are an attorney defending Rescuers, you have no choice in such circumstances. The deck is stacked in favor of maintaining an immoral law, and you are compelled to play the game according to these phony rules—that is, unless you are California Attorney Cyrus Zal.

An Iranian-born Christian,[2] Cyrus Zal demonstrates the fortitude of St. John the Baptist when pleading in the courts for the pre-born and for his clients, the defenders of the pre-born. In a judicial system which has always and heretofore traditionally pursued truth in all other types of cases, Zal has the audacity to voice it when the matter concerns abortion.[3]

For instance, this outspoken crusader was sentenced to 290 days for contempt of court in El Cajon, California by Judge Larrie Brainard for using terms which bestowed humanity on the pre-born.[4]

"Judge Larrie Brainard wanted me to ignore the fact that the slaughter of unborn children was the central issue. . ." But Zal could not ignore the blood crying out. He refused to harden himself to follow Brainard's order to delete God and children from the record. "How long have you been in the baby-killing business?" he asked the head of security of the largest abortion mill chain in California. "What time do the first victims arrive?" he asked the clinic worker. To the cop, he directed, "Did you feel an obligation to protect the children who would be killed that day?"[5]

"Gagging" the truth about abortion in the U.S. courts is permissible, although anti-nuclear protesters in their defense cases may invoke the "necessity defense" and Communists promoting revolution are protected by freedom of speech.[6] The silencing of Pro-Life attorneys and their defendants is even more outrageous considering the extreme freedom of expression permitted in some so-called "art forms" that have been funded by the U.S. government. Examples of such "art forms" are those with child-porn motifs or sacrilegious exhibitions, such as a picture of a crucifix submerged in urine.

In a society bent on self-destruction by killing its posterity,

Cyrus Zal is a courageous voice for life in the hostile arena of the American courtroom. His weapon in this battle against "principalities and powers" of darkness is the Holy Bible. He boldly carries[7] and quotes from the Scriptures in the proceedings he is involved in.[8] It is ironic that this is frowned upon, considering that witnesses in our courts were once required to "swear in" with their hand on the Bible.

Proclaiming his faith in God, Cyrus Zal declares, "I trust the Lord—whatever He wants me to do. I feel the Holy Spirit guiding me in the courtroom."[9] Apparently graced with divine counsel and fortitude, he persists in citing the "necessity defense," even after judges forbid it.[10] Cyrus Zal affirms, "I cannot abrogate my responsibilities to humanity and to the Nuremberg Convention by following the court's instructions and admonitions. I believe I'd rather face contempt."[11]

Of Judge Brainard's sentence, Cyrus Zal served ten days in jail before being transferred to detention in the Work Furlough Center, where he spent an additional four months. After that, he was placed on the Electronic Surveillance Program (house arrest), which allowed him to work. Altogether, Attorney Zal served seven months and 10 days.

This crusader for life has no regrets for his sacrifice. On the contrary, he believes, "It's an honor to be in jail for the unborn baby"[12] and to expose this "crime against humanity"[13] for all to see.

More recently, Attorney Zal has been in the process of appealing his case and other Rescue cases to the U.S. Supreme Court. His latest project is the creation of the screen play for a feature-length movie. Although this production will have a powerful pro-life message, Cyrus Zal promises that it will be entertainment rather than simply message.

Attorney Cyrus Zal, who persists in invoking the "necessity defense" in defending Pro-Life Rescuers. Attorney Zal has served over 7 months in jail, Work Furlough Center and on house arrest for "contempt of court"—that is, for his courageous and common-sense stand in dealing with defendants whose "crime" was that they were attempting to save babies.

18
Mother Teresa

The streets of Calcutta, India are crowded with countless homeless people. Some are lying in the gutters, sick or dying, with no one to help them. Others are children, orphaned or abandoned. These souls are the poorest of the poor. With Calcutta's overwhelming mass of human misery and poverty, pro-abortionists might seemingly have a case for population control through abortion to prevent more "unwanted" people from being born. But there is another answer.

Located at 54A Acharya J. Chandra Bose in Calcutta are the Missionaries of Charity—an order of sisters who bring light and hope to the city. They literally pick up the suffering and dying people off the streets and carry them to a place of refuge, where, if they are to die, they can do so with dignity and human compassion. These "Angels of Mercy" also run an orphanage and assist in the adoption of children.

The founder and leader of this religious order is an 80-year-old sister named Mother Teresa, who is known, respected and loved throughout the world. Many believe she is a living Saint.

Winner of the 1979 Nobel Peace Prize, she has addressed the United Nations and received honor from various heads of state. In addition to her motherhouse in Calcutta, Mother Teresa has established similar missions throughout the world.

Her compassion knows no ethnic or national boundaries.

In harmony with her international perspective, she believes that abortion is the greatest threat to world peace. Although she is very familiar with the overcrowding of slums and ghettos, Mother Teresa does not advocate abortion as a solution. Quite the contrary, this saintly woman values the sanctity of each life. Adoption is her answer to "unwanted" children, by making them wanted by loving adoptive parents. Of course, no child is unwanted by God.

On this burning issue, Mother Teresa tells us:

> I think that the cry of children who are assassinated before they come into the world is surely heard by God. Jesus has said that we are much more important in the eyes of His Father than the grass, the birds, or the lilies of the field. He also said that if the Father cares for all these things, much more will He care for His own life in us. Jesus cannot deceive us. Life is the greatest gift of God to human beings, and man has been created in the image of God. Life belongs to God, and we have no right to destroy it.[1]

The author has direct personal experience with Mother Teresa's Pro-Life endeavors. At his request, the "Angel of Calcutta" wrote a letter to his local State's Attorney, pleading with him to dismiss charges against 108 Rescuers who had attempted to save innocent life by peacefully blocking a local abortion mill entrance. Mother Teresa responded with the following letter to the Winnebago County State's Attorney:

> Dear Mr. Paul Logli,
>
> In February and April, 1989 some people tried to rescue babies about to be killed at an abortion clinic at Rockford.
>
> These people were upholding the law of God, which is above the law of man.

I request you in the name of God and as a fellow Roman Catholic, to dismiss charges of criminal trespass and of resisting or obstructing a police officer.

I will pray that you will have the courage to stand for, and protect, the beautiful gift of God, the preborn child. I know you will need courage to dismiss the charges, but I will ask Our Lady to be a mother to you and to help you.

Do not be afraid—do it for the glory of God and the good of the unborn child.

May Mary, Mother of Jesus, be a mother to you now.

Let us pray.

> God bless you,
> Mother Teresa, m.c.[2]

The State's Attorney continued to prosecute Pro-Life Rescuers rather than honoring Mother Teresa's plea.

Admittedly, it is difficult to jeopardize one's career for righteousness. A State's Attorney would risk substantial criticism and persecution if he dismissed charges against Rescuers, since he is also sworn to uphold the statutes of the land. However, in this post-Christian, neo-pagan era, America needs courageous leaders who put God's law first—and, moreover, are willing to sacrifice their professional standings for the truth. If our nation becomes governed by career politicians concerned primarily about re-election, we will be devoid of a moral foundation based on transcendent values.

Throughout history, civilizations without morality have declined to extinction. To escape this fate America will have to uphold law that is based on transcendent truth from God. This truth comes not only from the Christian Revelation, but is also found in the works of Cicero and Plato.

Mother Teresa's firm stand against abortion even amid the hardships and terrible crowding of India is a powerful witness to the sanctity of human life.

Mother Teresa, the "Angel of Calcutta," whose labors for the destitute, the abandoned and the dying have become world-famous. Even after living for years among "the poorest of the poor" in the misery of Calcutta, Mother Teresa does not hesitate to affirm that "Life belongs to God, and we have no right to destroy it."

19

Judie Brown

A young couple attending a small parish church with their three-month-old son in 1969 had their inner peace shaken on that Sunday morning as their pastor warned of their state's attempt to liberalize an existing abortion law. Recently, that same wife asserted, "I will never forget that sermon, and I could hardly know then just how thoroughly Father Willenburgh's words would change my life."[1]

In what turned out to be a prophetic statement, this priest predicted the holocaust of abortion that has followed and which is held up to the world as a solution to the problems of our increasingly permissive society. He also forewarned the congregation about the danger of euthanasia that would follow in abortion's train. Citing abortion as indicative of our moral decline, he called ours "a world without God!"[2]

Alarmed by this homily, the couple almost immediately began to work against their state's expansion of its child-killing laws. Although they tried to inform other people of the need to prevent this turn of events, the state of Washington eventually passed the pro-death legislation anyway.

Since that time, this couple, Judie and Paul Brown, have devoted themselves wholeheartedly to the Pro-Life cause. Today Judie Brown is President of the nation's largest Pro-Life activist organization, American Life League. As its

Chief Executive Officer, Paul Brown helps her manage the organization and has also founded the Life Amendment Political Action Committee.

Cooperating together as a loving team, they have authored the book *Choices* (Magnificat Press), which reveals the truth about abortion-related issues and recommends ways to counteract this evil.

Dedicated to a God-centered approach to fighting abortion, the League prays each morning for divine assistance to promote their Pro-Life actions and to meet the needs of those they serve.

They envision their work as a wheel, with God being the hub and the spokes being composed of a variety of vital projects:

1) *Education:* They supply appropriate Pro-Life materials for all needs.

2) *Lobbying:* They instruct voters on how most effectively to impact public officials.

3) *Non-violent Direct Action:* They provide specialized materials for those involved in picketing and protesting.

4) *Sidewalk Counseling:* They supply specific handbooks for this life-saving intervention.

5) *Crisis Pregnancy Counseling:* They assist crisis pregnancy centers throughout the nation.

6) *Post-Abortion Counseling:* They advise groups involved in "healing" women who are grieving after the murder of their pre-born children.

7) *Adoption:* They help to facilitate this alternative to abortion.

8) *Project Compassion:* They fight for the right of the elderly, the disabled and the terminally ill to continue living.

9) *Political Action:* They publish a series of "lessons" on lobbying, which can turn an average American into a "political wizard."[3]

It would be a big job to describe fully the entire range of American Life League's programs; it is sufficient to say, rather, that it is the most comprehensive organization of its kind, consisting of some 250,000 members. Under the American Life League structure are groups like Teens' American Life League (founded by Judie's dynamic daughter, Christy), Executives for Life, and Athletes for Life.

> The scope of the American Life League reflects the concern of Mrs. Judie Brown for all human beings "at risk." Not just a group battling against the horrors of abortion, American Life League has become widely known as the foremost champion of the rights of handicapped newborns and was instrumental in the development of "Baby Doe" regulations. Similarly, American Life League is working to protect the elderly and dependent from the threat of active euthanasia foreshadowed by the growing "right-to-die" movement.[4]

On the forefront of the Pro-Life movement, Judie Brown is sought by the media as a highly regarded spokesperson. She has appeared on *20/20,* CBS's *60 Minutes, The Phil Donahue Show* and *Oprah,* as well as on numerous radio and other television talk shows. Judie is not only straightforward in proclaiming the truth about life issues, but she is also very caring.

In addition, her editorials have been published in a wide variety of magazines and newspapers, including *The Washington Post, USA Today, The New York Post,* and *The New York City Tribune.*

Unity 90, a monumental Pro-Life event, was organized by American Life League. From June 28 through July 1, 1990, Right-to-Life advocates convened in Chicago to hear nationally renowned leaders in the movement "share experiences and ideas"[5] for winning the abortion battle.

Pro-Life viewers across the nation participated in this historic meeting on June 30 via a satellite video conference. Included among the special guest speakers were Cardinal John J. O'Connor, Archbishop of New York; Dr. Jerry Falwell, President of Liberty University; Joe Scheidler, founder and Executive Director of Pro-Life Action League; Beverly McMillan, M.D., former abortionist; Judge Robert and Mrs. Mary Ellen Bork; Hon. Henry Hyde, U.S. Congressman; Father Paul Marx, founder and President of Human Life International; Jeannie Hill, R.N., of Sidewalk Counselors for Life, Inc.; and Nellie Gray, Esq., of March for Life.

More than a workshop, Unity 90 was a celebration of life for an estimated one million people. "The Pro-Life message was proclaimed in words, images and song by some of the most admired figures in the worlds of religion, politics, sports and entertainment. . ."[6]

The American Life League publishes *All About Issues,* an extremely informative magazine. It addresses a wide variety of topics, ranging from teen chastity to the voting records of Congressmen and Senators, from black Pro-Life leaders to "licensed back alley" abortions, from organizing Life-Chains to honoring deceased Pro-Life leaders—that is, to virtually the entire spectrum of issues supporting life.

It is probably safe to say that the Pro-Life cause would not have progressed to its present state without Judie Brown and the American Life League. Zealously enthusiastic and deeply compassionate, Mrs. Brown is unswerving in her commitment to the pre-born.

When the American Life League celebrated its tenth anniversary in 1989, Judie Brown affirmed her total dedication: "I admire so very much those leaders in our work who consistently say: 'No Compromise.' For, after all, who are we to decide which babies should live and which should die?"[7]

Judie and Paul Brown have three children of their own. Judie is a Roman Catholic and was educated at the University of Los Angeles and the New York Management School.

Judie Brown, who was suddenly awakened to the horror of abortion during a sermon one Sunday morning in 1969. Judie now heads the nation's largest Pro-Life activist organization, American Life League, which is involved in numerous Pro-Life projects including promoting legislation to protect the unborn, the handicapped and the elderly.

20
Congressman Henry Hyde

In a time when many politicians are "selling out" their principles for political expediency, United States Congressman Henry Hyde of Illinois (6th District) is a source of hope and inspiration for the Pro-Life movement. He is best known for the 1976 "Hyde Amendment," which he sponsored and which was voted into law and which now prevents Medicaid recipients from using federal funds for abortions.

In his argument for the pre-born, Representative Hyde has declared, "If you believe that human life is deserving of due process of law. . .then you cannot in logic and conscience help fund the execution of these innocent, defenseless human lives."[1]

Pro-abortionists argue that this type of legislation deprives poor women of the right to terminate their pregnancies; whereas, those financially better off have access to child-killing. However, low-cost abortion-on-demand has been available since 1973, and there is no proof that poverty has in any way lessened abortions among the poor since that time. Furthermore, one wonders how much God will bless a nation's entire economy while it is killing the most vulnerable and defenseless of its posterity.

Congressman Henry Hyde has suffered persecution for taking his stand for life. Pro-abortion groups such as Planned

Parenthood and the American Civil Liberties Union have schemed to prove that his legislation was a violation of the separation of church and state, because of the Congressman's religious affiliation.

In a clandestine operation, attorneys for these organizations hired a detective to spy on Congressman Hyde while he attended a Mass for the pre-born. Notes were even taken to document the case against him while he read from the Scriptures during the Mass. However, their efforts to discredit him did not prevail in the courts.

This man, who is deeply imbued with Christian values, continues to uphold the rights of the pre-born. He was one of the principal speakers at the gigantic April, 1990 Rally for Life in Washington, D. C. and at the Unity 90 video conference in June of the same year. Wherever two or three prominent national Pro-Life leaders are summoned, Congressman Hyde will likely be there.

In 1977 he spoke the following words of encouragement to the Maryland Right-to-Life Convention. This timeless message applies to today's heroes involved in any aspect of the Pro-Life movement:

> When the time comes, as it surely will, when we face that awesome moment, the Final Judgment, I've often thought, as Fulton Sheen wrote, that it is a terrible moment of loneliness. You have no advocates, you are there alone, standing before God—and a terror will rip your soul like nothing you can imagine. But I really think that those in the Pro-Life movement will not be alone. I think there'll be a chorus of voices that have never been heard in this world but are heard beautifully and clearly in the next world—and they will plead for everyone who has been in this movement. They will say to God, "Spare him, because he loved us"; and God will look at you and say, not, "Did you succeed?" but, "Did you try?"[2]

Congressman Henry Hyde, responsible for the 1976 "Hyde Amendment," which prevents Medicaid recipients from using federal funds for abortions. Congressman Hyde has suffered persecution from pro-abortion groups for his Pro-Life stand.

21

Bishop Austin Vaughan

Because of its official Pro-Life stand, the Roman Catholic Church is the institution traditionally associated with protection of the pre-born. However, the degree of courage and commitment of New York's Auxiliary Bishop Austin Vaughan is outstanding. Laying his body and his reputation on the line, this prelate has participated in blocking abortion-clinic entrances in Operation Rescues. In his efforts to save lives, he has incurred fines and jail sentences, in addition to subjecting himself to possible criticism from the religious community. The author had the privilege of meeting Bishop Vaughan in 1989 and believes him to be deeply blessed with one of the true characteristics of a holy man—total dedication—yet, he is also imbued with a loving sense of humor, and his deep interior joy is a witness to the great dignity of human life.

Because of his commitment to the Pro-Life cause, Bishop Vaughan is often an honored speaker at Pro-Life rallies. When he speaks, he proclaims that individuals are unique and precious. Believing that each person is a part of God's plan, he asserts that no one has a right to interfere with that person's right to life.

Bishop Vaughan is alarmed at the complacency which people demonstrate toward the whole abortion issue. He voices special concern about the non-involvement of public officials and the clergy. With an estimated 26 million people having been killed by abortion since 1973, he views this crime as a greater tragedy in numerical terms than the Nazi holocaust of World War II or even than the total American war dead.

Along with the various Scriptural injunctions to love our neighbor, the prelate also cites the imperative we have to live together as "family." As a member of the human community, every single person should be allowed to make his or her own special contribution to life. Except in self-defense—and that as a last resort in a threatening situation—no one, he declares, has the right to take another person's life. Bishop Vaughan fears that the general acceptance of abortion by our culture will soon lead to euthanasia, as well as to the slaughter of those who are somehow "unproductive" in our utilitarian-oriented society. A person cannot help thinking of the elderly and the handicapped as being included in this category.

In justifying his participation in various Rescue Operations, Bishop Vaughan cites Divine Law as being above civil law because God forbids the taking of innocent human life. When he "breaks laws," such as those against trespassing, during his Rescue activities, Bishop Vaughan does not believe that he is truly committing a crime.

In addition to placing his body on the line to save lives, Bishop Vaughan also offers prayer support at Rescues. His interests and activities for life also extend beyond our national borders and include nations such as Australia and The Netherlands, where he has also been active.

Most recently, Bishop Vaughan has come out in support of an innovative and successful new way to get the Pro-Life message into the hands of college students, who often have never heard it.[1] The Human Life Alliance (HLA) of Redondo Beach, California has developed a large, 12-page, full-color Pro-Life brochure for insertion into campus newspapers as a paid "advertising supplement." The brochure gives phone numbers and locations of alternatives to abortion, plus providers of all other pregnancy needs, in the specific local area. A "test-run" (22,000 copies) was done at UCLA on May 12, 1992. Many babies and mothers have already been saved from abortion by this means, and HLA hopes to reach one million students in the next 12 months. (The cost at a large university of 10,000 students would be about $1,500.)

Bishop Vaughan states, "We now have a tool that *really works*—and it's ideal for college students."[2] He is asking for prayers and financial gifts so that HLA can spread this life-saving effort to schools across the nation.

Bishop Austin Vaughan, who has courageously participated in Operation Rescue, incurring fines and jail sentences for his efforts to save lives. Bishop Vaughan cites Divine Law as being above civil law; he states that God forbids the taking of innocent human life.

22

Pastor Matt Trewhella

God worked in a mysterious way when He selected a former juvenile delinquent to head one of the most effective Rescue groups in the nation.

When he was a teenager, Pastor Matt Trewhella broke the law and was arrested as a member of a Detroit street gang. As an adult, he continues to be arrested. However, this time he is upholding God's law by saving babies from slaughter at the abortion mills.

Founder of the Milwaukee "Operation Rescue," Rev. Trewhella is not a pastor of a grand church with a magnificent sanctuary. Instead, he presides over a smaller congregation in a humble setting at Mercy Seat Church in Milwaukee. As usual, God uses what the world considers insignificant to confound the "wise."

Through his Pro-Life apostolate, this 32-year-old preacher has spearheaded the closing of a Milwaukee abortuary and the saving of scores of babies. He was propelled into Pro-Life work in the summer of 1988 after viewing pictures of pre-born children.

When doing sidewalk counseling, Pastor Matt heard of the Rescue efforts in Atlanta. He courageously decided to organize a group in Milwaukee. Since that time, he has participated in over 100 Rescues and has been arrested numerous times on minor "technical" charges for saving babies. Hundreds of Pro-Lifers have participated in his larger Rescues, which involve sidewalk counseling and picketing, in addition to blocking the abortuary entrance.

After being active in the Rescue movement for a period of time, Pastor Matt saw the need for a full-time missionary group for children in the womb. He subsequently founded Missionaries to the Preborn. This organization is composed of believers who, on a regular basis, heroically sacrifice careers and home life to block abortuary entrances.

Although he is a humble man and does not seek glory for himself, Reverend Trewhella has made headlines. In 1991 he publicly tore up an injunction against his group, and persisted in his efforts to save lives. In the same year, his organization played a key role in the "Tollway Rescue." In this operation, Pro-Lifers surrounded, lay down in front of, and otherwise prevented mobility of the car of abortionist Dr. Aleksander Jakubowski, who was on his way to Milwaukee from Illinois to kill pre-born children. The Illinois State Police, using a huge amount of manpower, eventually were able to provide the abortionist a cleared way. However, the Rescue did delay him, and, as usual, he was greeted at the Milwaukee abortuary by "Missionaries" blocking the entrance.

The Missionaries in Milwaukee experienced one of their most moving episodes on January 24, 1992. A young man and the mother of his pre-born child arrived at a Milwaukee abortion mill. When they failed to gain access because of Missionaries present, they turned away. At this point, the father gave the "thumbs up" to the Missionaries and thanked them. But as the couple reached the street corner, the father's hopes were dashed. The presence of the Milwaukee Police Department prompted the mother to walk back toward the killing center. The officers then proceeded to whisk her into a squad car and escort her to the abortuary.

After the police began arresting the Missionaries, the father joined the Missionaries to perform the last act of love for his child. The Missionaries began to pray with this man for his baby's life. He told the Rescuers that he had pleaded with his girlfriend not to kill their child and that he had expressed to her his willingness to care for the baby. This man was soon arrested by police, who knew him to be the father. In jail he later shared this with the Missionaries: "I don't know why any man wouldn't do what I did. The killing of an innocent person is never a solution." The father was released from jail that evening with a court date to answer for his "crime."

Pastor Matt is a stirring speaker and an eloquent writer for the Pro-Life cause. He is much sought after to address rallies and other Pro-Life events because he forcefully exposes the truth about abortion. The following statement reflects his resolve and summarizes his determination in protecting pre-born children: "If we, as the church, do not attempt to protect children threatened by abortion, we are laughingstocks to every devil in Hell and a grief to every just man who lives."[1]

The author has rescued under the direction of Pastor Matt half a dozen times. I have the utmost confidence in his ability as a leader and his dedication to the cause. Rev. Trewhella's shining example has been one of the greatest sources of strength and inspiration to me. Through his radical obedience to God's law over man's law, he has truly made a difference.

Monsignor Emmenegger, Pastor of St. Mary's Church in the Milwaukee suburb of Elm Grove, is an area clergyman who supports Pastor Matt and the Milwaukee Rescue. He describes Rev. Trewhella as "a friend of mine since his earliest days of work with Operation Rescue." This Catholic priest further declares, "I have been privileged to share in that project. I have a deep respect for the courage and dedication of Pastor Matt. His gentle manner belies his strong spirit and fierce devotion to protecting the unborn."[2]

Rev. Trewhella is himself a husband and father. His wife Clara supports his Pro-Life activities and is also a Rescuer.

Pastor Matt recently challenged the acceptance of birth control by Protestant churches. In a July, 1992 exclusive in

Life Advocate magazine, he called the Protestant acceptance of birth control "heretical." He cited Scripture passages to support his contention, such as "Be fruitful and multiply" from *Genesis*. Pastor Matt went on to relate the anti-child mentality behind birth control to the rationale behind abortion.

Reverend Trewhella and his wife are eagerly awaiting the birth of their third child.

*   *   *

Keeping updated on Pastor Matt's life-saving work is a challenge. As of September, 1992, he was incarcerated in the Milwaukee County House of Corrections for protecting the innocent.

Throughout the summer of 1992, Pastor Matt had rallied thousands of believers to stand for life at Milwaukee abortuaries. In the month of August alone, nine babies were confirmed saved.[3]

In one of the most spectacular demonstrations of love for the pre-born, 10,000 Christians gathered at the Mecca arena in Milwaukee on August 7, 1992 to repent for atrocities in their city. Among them were 168 pastors, who led the people in prayer.[4]

On the following day, 6,000 believers witnessed to their convictions at Wisconsin Women's Health Center, a local abortuary. There 536 adults and 87 juveniles were arrested for interposing their bodies to prevent the "doctor" from practicing his gruesome trade.[5] God honored the courageous act of these Pro-Lifers: No babies were killed that day.

The Rescue was the largest single local Rescue in the history of the movement.[6]

Pastor Matt Trewhella, whose Missionaries to the Preborn are now one of the most effective Rescue groups in the nation. Their series of Rescues in Milwaukee in the summer of 1992 rallied thousands of believers and saved many babies.

23

Jamie Tellier

A middle school in Plano, Texas ordered a student not to distribute Pro-Life material on campus. Administrators of the school maintained that it was "graphic and explicit." Furthermore, they charged that the literature disrupted classes and that it was inappropriate for children of that age. At the same time, the administration of this school did not consider condom demonstrations inappropriate.

However, 14-year-old Jamie Tellier continued her mission to educate other students and to save babies. Even when the school placed her in the Temporary Reassignment Adjustment Center, a program for students with behavioral problems, she was not deterred. "I feel the babies are so important," asserted Jamie.

According to this courageous young Catholic girl, she distributes Pro-Life literature between classes and before or after school, but only to students who request it. She also provides adoption information to pregnant girls who are considering abortion.

Her efforts have been fruitful. Jamie reports that she has persuaded several girls not to abort their babies and has encouraged them to choose the adoption option. In addition, she counsels those who have aborted their children.

Jamie frequently exposes the lies inherent in the abortion

industry by going to abortion mills with her peers who are contemplating abortion. She points out how the staff does not give all the facts about the procedure, about fetal development, or about other options.

Jamie began her Pro-Life apostolate at age 12 when she saw a photo of "Baby David," a decapitated aborted baby. She has been supported by Texans United For Life and by picketers marching in front of her school on her behalf. Jamie is the co-founder of TRUTH (Texans Rescuing Unborn Tiny Humans) and has rescued with adult groups, being arrested on many occasions. Fr. Norman Weslin of the Lambs of Christ and Pastor Matt of The Missionaries to the Preborn (Milwaukee) are among those with whom she has exercised her apostolate. In addition, Jamie speaks to youth groups, high school assemblies and church congregations.

Jamie's parents, Cliff and Laura, are behind her Pro-Life activities and openly voice support for her. As a matter of fact, they fought a federal injunction which the school was seeking against Jamie. Jamie's mother is herself a Rescuer.

As with other devout Christians, Jamie's Pro-Life work is nourished by daily prayer and Scriptural meditation, with the Rosary as a foundation of her spiritual life.

Although Jamie is only in her early teens, her actions serve as an example to adults who may not yet have the courage to stand up for their Pro-Life convictions. Hopefully, her witness will inspire more involvement from people of all ages.

Jamie encourages letters from other teens who wish to join the Pro-Life apostolate. They are invited to write to her at 2501 Evans Drive, Plano, Texas 75075.

Jamie Tellier, a 14-year-old Texas girl who has braved harassment from school officials for passing out Pro-Life literature on campus. Jamie has also participated in numerous Rescues, being arrested many times. Jamie says, "I feel the babies are so important."

24

Monica Migliorino Miiler

In 1976, a devout Roman Catholic at Southern Illinois University made a retreat at the Newman Center. This spiritual event led her into the Pro-Life movement, a movement to which she was soon to dedicate her life.

Monica Migliorino eventually participated in her first Rescue on March 11, 1978 at Concord Medical Services in Chicago. She was arrested for interposing her body between the babies scheduled for execution and the killing doctor.

Between 1978 and 1985 Monica organized further Rescues in Chicago. Becoming experienced in sidewalk counseling, she persuaded many women to save their babies instead of aborting them.

In September, 1985, this servant of God's littlest ones moved to Milwaukee to study for her Ph.D. in Theology at Marquette University. There she continued her Pro-Life apostolate by founding Citizens for Life, an activist organization, in January of 1986. Furthering her commitment to the cause, Monica led the first Milwaukee Rescue on March 8, 1986 at the Bread and Roses Women's Health Center, emerging soon after as a respected Pro-Life leader.

In March, 1988, Monica propelled many formerly apathetic people into the Pro-Life movement when she exposed an atrocity that subsequently received national attention: A Milwaukee pet cemetery was incinerating the bodies of aborted babies along with the remains of dead cats and dogs.

In the same year, Monica and Citizens for Life helped retrieve the remains of about 5,000 aborted babies from the loading dock of Vital Med, a Northbrook, Illinois pathology lab, where they had been shipped from eight different states. The bodies of these infants were in the trash awaiting pickup. Over the seven-month duration of this sad project, Monica helped arrange for a number of burials for these victims at locations throughout the nation. Twelve hundred were buried at Holy Cross Cemetery in Milwaukee on September 10, 1988. Five hundred persons attended a wake for these infants; 100 cars lined up for two miles for a funeral procession to the cemetery with the hearses bearing the children's remains.[1] A year later, Monica directed the dedication of a monument at this site.

In 1989, Monica was added to the list of defendants in the NOW v. Scheidler class-action lawsuit. The reasons she was included in this litigation were 1) her retrieval of the dead babies, 2) her rescuing and 3) her persuading a Milwaukee landlord not to rent to a local abortion center.

Monica was also sentenced to a nine-month jail term for a June 9, 1989 Rescue at Imperial Medical Services in Milwaukee. This case is on appeal.

Monica was awarded her Ph.D. in Systematic Theology from Marquette University in May, 1991. She is now a part-time lecturer at Marquette. Her writings include published articles on the Pro-Life movement. Among them are "Pet Lawn Cemetery and the Last Work of Mercy" in *Fidelity* (July/August, 1988); "Abortion Battles Ahead: Operation Rescue Gets Headlines—Does It Also Save Lives?" in *Crisis* (September, 1989); "Severed Ties: How Abortion Dissolves Feminine Authority," in *Crisis* (November, 1991); and "The Burial of the Aborted Unborn," in *Homiletic and Pastoral Review* (August-September, 1989).

Monica is married to Edmund Miller and is the mother of a daughter, Bernadette. She continues to champion the cause of children in the womb. Her strong conviction is reflected in the following statement:

> A certain pro-life poster reads: "When one child dies, the whole world mourns. When a million children die, the world doesn't care." This slogan contains a great deal of wisdom. That we could be concerned about the one and bypass the one million goes to the heart of the pro-abortion ethic. The pro-life ethic, and I should say really the Catholic ethic, believes in the utterly individual and unique beauty of each person.
>
> Abortion is not only about denying the unborn their God-given right to life. Abortion is equally as evil because it disintegrates human relationships. The plight of the aborted child is not simply that he is killed, but that, cast from his mother's womb, he is horribly and frighteningly *alone*.
>
> Pro-life work is about calling human beings back into relation—about calling them to be a radical healing balm on the death chamber alienation that abortion represents.[2]

In this era of academic theologians who rationalize evils like abortion by "intellectualizing" the Gospel and the teachings of the Church, Monica Miller is a standard-bearer for the truth. She not only teaches the authentic message of Jesus Christ, but also lays down her life for the most helpless of her friends—pre-born children.

Monica Miller with Fabian, a baby saved from abortion through her sidewalk counseling efforts. Monica is one of the defendants in a class-action suit by NOW (National Organization of Women); she is being sued for various Pro-Life activities, including helping to retrieve the bodies of 5,000 aborted infants from a trash dump in order to arrange a Christian burial for them.

25
Conrad Wojnar

The abortion industry's survival depends on denial of the truth and upon deception. Exposing the truth about it is very difficult and can be extremely costly in our present pro-death culture.

Conrad Wojnar, Director of Des Plaines Pro Life, located in the Chicago area, is enduring severe persecution for his valiant deeds in upholding the dignity of the pre-born. This father of six children is being sued by Molly Yard and the National Organization of Women (N.O.W.), mainly for having had the "audacity" to help assure a Christian burial for over 5,000 aborted infants. These children's bodies were originally destined to be disposed of in a garbage dump.

Based on a twisted sense of justice, the lawsuit alleges that Conrad is a "racketeer." The Racketeer Influenced and Corrupt Organizations Act (RICO) was originally designed to be a deterrent to organized criminal activities, but is now being used against Conrad. Because RICO provides for triple damages, losing the case would be devastating for him and his family.

A judge dismissed the suit in 1991, ruling that Conrad was motivated by Pro-Life principles rather than by economic interests. Furthermore, he called the lawsuit "nonsensical." However, N.O.W. has appealed the case.

Conrad Wojnar's Pro-Life apostolate was founded upon his love of God and devotion to the Blessed Virgin Mary. He and his wife Linda had been members of the Legion of Mary, a Catholic organization which aims to bring all men to Christ through Mary. Then in May of 1982 they consecrated themselves to Mary in the way taught by St. Louis De Montfort. Thus they turned over to Mary all their spiritual and material possessions so as to allow her to unite them closely with her Son more quickly and more surely.

Shortly after that, Conrad and his wife began to receive Pro-Life information. The following January, he viewed .a Pro-Life movie which disturbed him deeply. According to Conrad, "I hadn't ever realized the extent of the abortion disaster. I had never fully realized the methods and the false arguments used in destroying the lives of babies." His participation in an interfaith prayer vigil and 24-hour prayer chain for the pre-born inspired him to take action.

In July of 1983, he founded the first Des Plaines Pro Life office. This was a part-time educational program. Next came what Conrad calls a "turning point." He attended a Pro-Life meeting organized by the Pearson Institute, a national program for initiating counseling centers to save babies from abortion. He was persuaded to set up a center and selected a site near the "infamous" Albany abortion mill in Chicago, which made a practice of doing late-term abortions.

Conrad still needed to work at another full-time job to support his family. However, with an all-volunteer staff, the center assisted 20 clients the first month. In September of 1985, Mr. Wojnar withdrew the $20,000 he had accumulated in his pension fund so that he was able to begin a full-time ministry. This was a difficult step because the couple had just had their fourth child.

Since that time, Des Plaines Pro Life has grown in number and scope of services and in professionalism. Its services include four counseling centers in the Chicago area (located adjacent to abortion mills), a Family Room Resale Shop/

Resource Center supplying clothing, food and furniture (for example, hundreds of cribs have been refurbished by volunteers and put back into active service), and a multi-purpose administrative and printing center. The official publication of Des Plaines Pro Life is *Vigil Newsletter*.

Over the years Conrad has continually had to scramble for financial survival; he has learned more and more to rely on Divine Providence on a daily basis, especially through the intercession of the Blessed Virgin Mary and that of St. Jude, Patron of Impossible Cases. In fact, Conrad states that "the first thing we did back in 1983 was to organize an around-the-clock prayer vigil, emphasizing the Eucharist and the Rosary. We knew we couldn't accomplish anything without God's guiding hand." That prayer vigil continues today, with individuals signing up for 15-minute time slots once a week.

Of the over 400 women now counseled by the organization every month, most choose life. Conrad reports that seven to eight infants are saved per day, and the number is quickly growing. He estimates that Des Plaines Pro Life has been instrumental in saving 7,500 children so far. Lists of first names and birthdates of babies saved are periodically compiled and distributed by Des Plaines Pro Life to encourage its supporters. Conrad estimates that it costs about $250 to save a baby (not including such additional things as material help to needy mothers).[1]

The main tool for attracting pregnant women to the counseling centers is a full-page Yellow-Pages ad offering free pregnancy testing and "abortion-related services" at Des Plaines Pro Life's four "Women's Centers"; the ad runs ahead of the abortuary ads. The headlines simply inquire: "Considering abortion?" Although the organization's ads do not state that they are Pro-Life, Des Plaines Pro Life does not lie to clients. Initially withholding information is simply a method used to reach women in need. This is acceptable in a time of crisis, especially when a life is in danger.

Clients are always respected and are free to leave at any

time, but they rarely opt to leave before their situation is fully explored. They are shown a video presentation on abortion and fetal development, and they are personally counseled. All is done in an atmosphere of love. Fully 75% of the women eventually agree with the counselor that abortion is not the answer to their problem.

Conrad describes how this statistic is arrived at: "On an average day our counselors see 20 women. Twelve or 13 turn out to be pregnant, and 10 or 11 of the pregnant mothers are seeking an abortion. After providing full information to the abortion-bound mothers, seven or eight of them choose life for their babies—an almost unheard-of success rate, thank God."[2] Des Plaines Pro Life is saving more babies, here and now, than probably any other Pro-Life organization in the country.[3] Over 2,500 a year are now being saved.[4]

Conrad sees a huge and increasing need for the type of services provided by Des Plaines Pro Life (approximately 200 pre-born infants die of abortion in the Chicago metropolitan area each day),[5] and he hopes to open more Women's Centers in the future. The next location he is looking at is the Loop in downtown Chicago.

Conrad says, "What concerns me most in the pro-life movement is the attitude that the abortion battle will be won through human tactics. I'm convinced that the problem is much more serious than the lack of education about the evils of abortion. The fight to save babies is a spiritual battle." He sees the practice of contraception as undermining Americans' will to resist abortion: "The whole contraceptive mentality, which is much more pervasive than abortion, is withering away the moral resolve of Americans to fight abortion."

Conrad firmly opposes contraception. He believes it promotes fornication, promiscuity and an anti-baby mentality— with contraception being the "first line of defense against unwanted pregnancy" and abortion being the back-up system. For those with a need to space children or avoid pregnancy,

Des Plaines Pro Life advocates Natural Family Planning, which is based on periodic abstinence.

Even if abortion is made illegal, Des Plaines Pro Life plans to continue and to expand its role of helping mothers with alternatives to abortion. He firmly believes that hearts as well as laws must be changed before abortion is done away with.

Conrad and his organization welcome any support from others who wish to join them in this work of serving God, trusting to have the privilege of standing before Our Lord someday and saying: "We are useless servants. We have done no more than our duty."

Anyone wishing to help or who needs to be helped in this effort may call Des Plaines Pro Life at 312-794-1313.

Conrad Wojnar, founder of Des Plaines Pro Life. Using the Pearson method, their Women's Centers in Chicago are saving over 2,500 infants per year from abortion—7 or 8 per day. This amazing success is obtained through the constant prayers of supporters.

26

Governor Robert Casey
of Pennsylvania

This nation is in the midst of one of the greatest moral crises in its history. Abortion on demand has extinguished more lives than all of our wars combined. We are killing our posterity and denying the inalienable right to life guaranteed to all people by God and the United States Constitution.

The degradation of human life by abortion is a by-product of the greater and general breakdown of true Christian morality throughout Western Civilization. And in the area of family values, we are the witnesses of alarming increases in free-love, common-law marriage, infidelity, divorce, homosexuality, pornography, child abuse and wife abuse. The economic consequences alone of destroying the lives of 30 million pre-born children may not be realized for decades. Loss of jobs due to a lack of product demand, a declining school enrollment and a resulting deterioration of the educational system, and the depletion of future Social Security funds are only the most apparent. (And this is not to mention the many "subtle" chastisements Almighty God is sending us to warn us, as a society, of our sins—not the least of which is an ever-increasing poverty in a land that during the 1950's had a bigger economy than that of the rest of the world combined!)

If the United States does not change its present course, we will continue our downward spiral to social, moral and economic destruction. At this terrible moment in our history, we need great leaders and courageous statesmen to restore sanity.

Pennsylvania's Democratic Governor Robert Casey has emerged from the political fray as a true champion of life and true family values. Although the Democratic Party has caved in to its radical elements to become officially the "pro-choice" party, Governor Casey has challenged its pro-abortion platform.

He has not sold his party out. This leader describes himself as being "as strong a Democrat as there is."[1] However, he maintains that the national party does not speak for him on the abortion issue. In a statement to the Democratic National Committee, Governor Casey exhorts: "Our party has always been the voice of the powerless and the voiceless. They have been our natural constituency. Let us add to this list the most powerless and voiceless member of the human family: the unborn child."[2] He elaborates: "And I will go further and urge that, in fighting for life, we have a corresponding obligation to do all that we can to make life worth living for both mother and child."[3]

Governor Casey also believes that the abortion plank of the Democratic Party platform is out of touch with the values of the mainstream of American thought. He cites a 1990 Gallup Poll finding in which 77% of Americans polled said that abortion was the taking of human life. Affirming the results of this poll, Governor Casey declares, "I agree, and believe that taking the life of an innocent child is unjust. Abortion is the ultimate violence. Abortion on demand has, in my judgment, contributed significantly to an environment in our country in which life has become very cheap."[4]

Fortunately, this man of vision is not alone in his thinking. In 1989, in a letter to Party Chairman Ron Brown, 49 Democratic Members of Congress urged the Party to change its position. Furthermore, according to Governor Casey, 80 Democrats in the House have voted against their party's position. This is one-third of them. These figures contradict the message of those in the media who would have us conclude that Democrats are solidly "pro-choice." Nevertheless, it is true that Gov. Casey was "gagged" and denied the floor at the 1992 Democratic Presidential Convention, at which "choice" was proclaimed to be a woman's right.

The Governor has gone beyond verbally challenging his party. He signed a Pennsylvania law which outlines the following restrictions:

- Voluntary and Informed consent, with 24-hour waiting period, required from women before undergoing an abortion. (The information provided will let them know what they are getting into.)
- Parental consent required for minors under most situations.
- Notification of the husband, unless a woman's safety is at risk.
- Prohibition against sex-selection abortions.
- Prohibition against abortions after 24 weeks of gestational age, unless the life of the mother is at risk, and for limited health reasons.

The parental consent, voluntary and informed consent and spousal notification provisions were contested, then ruled upon by the United States Supreme Court.

Except for notification of the husband, these restrictions were upheld by the Court in its July, 1992 ruling in *Planned Parenthood v. Casey*, and they are now the law in Pennsylvania. However, in that ruling the Court specifically upheld its disastrous 1973 *Roe v. Wade* decision, citing "the court's legitimacy"[5] as reason to continue its pro-abortion stand.

The Pennsylvania statute is specific in protecting the interests of all potential victims of abortion. For example, it states, "No abortion shall be performed or induced except with the voluntary and informed consent of the woman upon whom the abortion is to be performed or induced."[6]

This provision is aimed partly at women such as the wife who fears a beating by her "old man" if she does not get rid of the child in her womb, and the frightened teenage girl whose parents are forcing her into having an abortion. The Pennsylvania law represents an attempt to give some protection to women such as these, and to others also who would otherwise allow their babies to be killed because they, the mothers, were under duress.

Refuting the false accusation that Pro-Lifers do not care about children already born, Pennsylvania is a model state in providing for children and families. The Commonwealth and its Governor have been acclaimed by such notables as NBC News anchorman Tom Brokaw and renowned pediatrician, Dr. T. Berry Brazelton.

Robert Casey is the father of eight children and the grandfather of fourteen. A high school valedictorian, he graduated *cum laude* from Holy Cross College in Worcester, Massachusetts with a degree in English. He received a scholarship from George Washington University Law School and was awarded his J.D. in 1956. In addition to having a history of public service, Robert Casey successfully ran a private law practice.

Governor Casey is certainly heroic in his efforts to steer his party in a righteous direction with regard to abortion. Like other famous men in history, this leading Pennsylvanian is taking a stand on a great moral issue. He is willing to go against the current trend of his party because of his deep convictions. Hopefully, more politicians will be inspired by Governor Casey and will follow his example of moral fortitude in the face of a tough choice—rather than caving in to radical elements for the sake of political expediency.

Democratic Governor Robert Casey of Pennsylvania, who has obtained several Pro-Life measures restricting abortion in his state. Gov. Casey believes that "taking the life of an innocent child is unjust," and that the Democratic Party, as the champion of the voiceless and powerless, must defend the unborn child. This great statesman was "gagged" at his party's 1992 presidential convention.

27
Shari Richard

The most powerful weapon of the Pro-Life movement is the truth. If the facts about abortion are made known to women, fewer of them will choose it as an option.

High Resolution Realtime Ultrasound is one of the greatest scientific breakthroughs to save the lives of pre-born infants. This technology enables one actually to see the pre-born child in the womb. When an expectant mother has the opportunity to view on an ultrasound screen the wondrous happenings inside her, she can have little doubt that a living child is present there and forming within her.

Ultrasonographer Shari Richard has created two marvelous videos detailing prenatal life. They are *Ultrasound: A Window to the Womb* (a 55-minute video for teens and adults) and *Ultrasound: Eyewitness to the Earliest Days of Life* (25 minutes, for all ages). Containing a touch of humor, these masterpieces display the escapades of our tiniest brothers and sisters: jumping, yawning and thumb-sucking are among the most remarkable.

These videos also capture the reactions of teenage girls in a classroom setting, who are amazed at the fascinating array of pre-natal functions and activities, as they view the Ultrasound video. Shari is shown pointing out to them significant biological facts, such as the heart beating only four weeks after conception and the defined sexual organs in later stages of pre-born development.

Between the colorful performances of the pre-born children and the awe of the girls, these presentations are very entertaining, in addition to being educational.

A Window to the Womb includes additional footage with Shari lecturing about the "stark reality" of abortion.

These videos are a must for schools, churches, hospitals and crisis pregnancy centers. It is unfortunate that abortion clinics are not mandated to show *A Window to the Womb* so that women will have more information before they make their "choice." It would be better yet if abortionists actually showed each client an Ultrasound of her own pre-born child. However, since Ultrasound is "user-dependent," requiring a trained eye to discern what is there, a woman would need to beware of deception by abortion profiteers who would misrepresent the image and still refer to her child as a "blob."

Shari has reported 90% success in saving infants with her Ultrasound machine. Armed with this sword of truth, she actually transports the unit to crisis pregnancy centers, where she shows each young woman an Ultrasound of her own baby, then gives her an Ultrasound video to take home for later viewing by herself, her parents and the father of the baby. These videos are so compelling that in Shari's first four months, every woman viewing them chose life. Seeing the actual living being inside of oneself provides for the ultimate in "informed consent"—or rather, after being truly informed, women decide *not* to consent to the death of their own flesh and blood.

A measure of the possible impact of the Ultrasound video is seen in the "pro-choice" reaction to it. On March 15, 1990, Shari attempted to testify to Congress against the so-called "Freedom of Choice Act" (HR25; S. 25). If passed into law, this bill would supersede any current state laws restricting abortion and would guarantee abortion on demand for the full nine months of pregnancy. When Shari asked to show Congress an Ultrasound video, she was "gagged" in a House subcommittee on the flimsy excuse that video testimony was inadmissible.

After Rep. Don Edwards refused the video presentation as testimony, Rep. James Sensenbrenner came forward declaring, "Never in my ten years on this subcommittee has there been an attempt to try to tell a witness how to present their testimony." He further stated, ". . .this is an attempt to censor a Pro-Life witness; video presentations are used all the time [and it is] not in the keeping of a subcommittee that is supposed to be concerned about civil rights and the freedom of speech."[1]

In an act of righteous indignation, Rep. Sensenbrenner stormed out of the hearing, declaring that the video could be shown in the corridor if necessary. This statesman wanted everyone to know what was being "gagged." The video was eventually shown in the hearing room, but by that time only those who were already Pro-Life were present.

In the Senate, where the Ultrasound video was allowed, Senator Orrin Hatch called Shari's testimony "the most powerful evidence brought before the government to date."[2]

An ultrasound video was eventually sent to every member of the U.S. Congress in an effort to dissuade them from voting for the "Freedom of Choice Act." These videos are so powerful and so instructive that the Pro-Life Director of the Catholic Diocese of Rockford, Illinois sent one to each of the over 60 Catholic grade and high schools and to every Catholic pastor in the diocese, for a total of over 150 videos.

The videos *A Window to the Womb* and *Eyewitness to the Earliest Days of Life* are available from Sound Wave Images, Inc., 2422 Harness, West Bloomfield, MI 48324. (Tel. No.: (313) 360-0743.) To arrange for an interview with Shari Richard, contact: Creative Media Resources, Don S. Otis, P. O. Box 1665, Standpoint, ID 83864. Phone & FAX: (208) 263-8055.

An article in a February, 1986 issue of *OB/GYN News* quoted a Dr. Sally Dorfman, who stressed the advisability

of turning the Ultrasound screen away from a patient while
her womb is being monitored. According to Dr. Dorfman,
"Seeing a blown-up moving image of the embryo she is carry-
ing can be distressing to a woman who is about to undergo
an abortion."[3]

These efforts to conceal reality are the core of the "pro-
choice" pathology. A woman *should* be distressed about the
safety of her child!

Shari's work in promoting life has roots in her own personal
story. At a vulnerable stage in her life during the early 1970's
Shari was victimized by two abortions. She was convinced that
inside her were merely "blobs of tissue." It was not until the
early 1980's, in Ultrasound school, that she discovered she
had killed two children. Since that time, Shari has sought
God's forgiveness and through her efforts with Ultrasound has
helped prevent other women from making the same mistake.
She accomplishes her mission by delighting viewers with the
beautiful mystery of life in the womb.

Along with being a defender of the pre-born's right to live,
Shari is opposed to the monstrous practice of "baby harvesting." This abomination involves using organs from aborted
babies for transplantation. The fact that the baby being "har-
vested" sometimes has to be alive during organ extraction
makes the procedure even more abominable.[4]

An effort currently underway in Congress to legalize federal funding for "baby harvesting" proves that our nation is
becoming increasingly pagan and barbaric. It is up to
believers to resist these evils and reverse our path to self-
annihilation.

Shari has received an excellent response when speaking to
groups about Ultrasound. On the last four occasions she
spoke, someone in the audience came forward with a check
to pay for an Ultrasound machine for the local Pro-Life
organization. The cost of such a machine is about $30,000.
On other occasions, Pro-Life physicians in the audience have
stood up to offer free Ultrasounds for pregnant women in

their office. Shari says, "Pro-Life doctors want to do something. They want to give more than money." She finds that doctors respect the professional quality of her work.

Shari has recently made over 10 Pro-Life "commercials" which are available for airing on local and national TV. The commercials are simple yet powerful as they show actual Ultrasound clips of pre-born babies jumping and moving about. One features the clear, strong heartbeat of a child at 28 days after conception. In these commercials Shari asks viewers to decide for themselves whether they are looking at a "blob" or a human being. These Pro-Life spots are fascinating—and very positive.

A VHS video which includes all these commercials may be obtained from Shari very reasonably. The sponsoring organization can dub in its name and phone number at the end of the message. Thereafter, the job is to raise funds to get the commercials on TV. Shari has found that when people view these commercials at fund-raisers, they are very excited and very willing to contribute generously to get them on TV.

Shari says, "I'm tired of preaching to the choir. We're not going to get the public to come to our Pro-Life meetings; the only way we're going to reach them is on the TV tube." She believes strongly that we need free Ultrasound in every single major city. Shari says, "I believe that abortion will become illegal as soon as the American people are educated on the fact that abortion kills human babies." She feels that people do not want to listen to someone else's moral and religious beliefs against abortion, but Ultrasound presents facts that cannot be disputed.

As Ultrasound becomes more widely known, it is virtually certain that many more babies will be saved and many mothers will be spared the tragedy of killing their own children. Their pregnancies will have the happy beginning of birth rather than the sad ending of abortion. Shari Richard herself has had three such beautiful beginnings as a wife and mother in West Bloomfield, Michigan.

Shari Richard, who learned in Ultrasound school that she had gotten rid of 2 real babies, rather than "blobs," when she had 2 abortions some years ago. As an ultrasonographer, Shari is meeting with a tremendous response to Ultrasound, by which a mother can actually view her own pre-born child within her womb. Shari says, "Ultrasound is saving thousands of lives."

28

Helen Doyle

Known as the "Forest City," Rockford, Illinois was once blanketed by so many huge Dutch Elm trees that it appeared as a green patch from an aerial view. However, the city was ravaged by the Dutch Elm Disease in the early 1960's, which destroyed much of its scenic ecological makeup. As devastating as this disease was, it turned out to be only an ominous forerunner of an even deadlier plague to follow—the destruction of human life through abortion-on-demand. Reforestation has now replaced most of the trees earlier lost because of the Dutch Elm parasite. And Rockford's impressive parks, its area lakes and its hilly landscape continue to produce a physically esthetic display. However, with all the area's splendor, the specter of abortion stands as a contradiction to the natural beauty of the city, because it attacks the very foundation of society—namely, human life.

The author is very familiar with the area's notorious abortuary at 1400 Broadway, where the landlord and his "security guard" hurl unrepeatable obscenities and bizarre accusations at Pro-Life picketers and sidewalk counselors. The author has personally witnessed this mockery of God and of religious values as an attempt to dissuade anyone from pleading for the pre-born, that they may not be slaughtered by the abortionist with the consent of their mothers.

Although Rockford is obviously a "church town," judging by its large number of churches, the religious community in general seems apathetic about child-killing—when one considers the small number of believers who are willing to demonstrate their horror over abortion by their presence at the death scene.

Granted that there are sincere individuals who are unsuited for direct confrontation and yet are committed to helping the pre-born through prayer, education and other means; nonetheless, the proportion of Christians who are personally involved in the Pro-Life movement in any way on a regular basis is consistently low. Although Rockford's apathy typifies other cities with abortuaries, it is a scandal in a town of its size, where hundreds of churches are listed in the telephone directory. It is a negative witness in an area which has traditionally prized itself as being a sanctuary of family values.

For six years a devoted woman named Helen Doyle has faithfully served God by her presence at the local abortuary on almost every day that it is open (three days per week). Arriving at its early-morning opening time, this 70-year-old grandmother is sometimes a solitary "soldier" at the clinic. She often has to conduct a lonely vigil until other Pro-Lifers arrive, being the only person present to plead for the babies. Furthermore, her age does not buffer her against the usual obscene verbal abuse directed at the Pro-Life demonstrators.

In previous years Helen was able to say a few last-minute words to women as they approached the building, but now, since a wall has been erected to keep the Pro-Life witnesses away from "customers," only the few who park on the street can be reached before they make their irrevocable decision. Helen says, "You don't know what to say, so you just say whatever comes into your head."

She has had many experiences and heard many tragic, true stories. She tells of the young father who was told to leave the abortion chamber because he persisted in trying to persuade his girlfriend to let their child live. Then he wanted to re-enter the building just to be silently present with her, but he was refused entrance, and so left the scene weeping. A young woman came to join the Pro-Life demonstrators, but spent the morning weeping out on the sidewalk; it turned out that she had had an abortion at this very clinic a year ago. The husband of a woman who was forced into having an abortion years ago as an unmarried teenager (she is now a Pro-Life counselor) says that still today, "We go through hell every March"—because his wife's sorrow and remorse surface again each year.

But there are joyful stories too. A couple entered the mill, but then exited after 20 minutes, looking absolutely radiant; they said, "God spoke to us in there. We're going to keep our baby." A woman who made a trip to the clinic was later seen at the local crisis pregnancy center, where she explained simply, "I just couldn't do it."

Helen Doyle is sustained by a deep faith in God, by attending daily Mass and by receiving Holy Communion. She realizes that she is never really alone at 1400 Broadway. Describing a "warm feeling" that overcame her on one occasion, Mrs. Doyle shows she is profoundly aware of God's presence with her, even when she has no human companionship. Serving both as a tribute and as an inspiration to Pro-Life sidewalk picketers everywhere, Helen Doyle's ongoing, often solitary witness is an affirmation to everyone in this movement—or who wants to help in this movement, in any way whatsoever, wherever he or she may be—that "It is better to light one candle than to curse the darkness!"

Helen Doyle's work is indeed typical in an heroic degree of the work which many tens of thousands of Pro-Life workers everywhere are doing, who, quietly and without recognition, sacrifice their time and their energy—yes, and often their reputation—in the cause of saving unborn babies from the holocaust of abortion. If it were not for the countless Helen Doyles of this world, who make up the rank and file of the Pro-Life movement, there would be no Pro-Life movement! Granted this great movement could never ever have existed without the tremendously talented, varied and self-sacrificing leadership raised up by God in defense of Life and outlined briefly (and admittedly, not all-inclusively) in this little book; yet, honor must needs be paid to the Helen Doyles of our effort, for they are the backbone and sinew and muscle of this movement. Without them, there would be no Pro-Life movement; there would be no one to follow the leadership of those courageous people who have sacrificed so much to take us so far. So finally, in the person of Helen Doyle, a completely self-sacrificing and dedicated Pro-Lifer, who never in the world thought of receiving recognition for her effort, this author would like to pay a humble and profound tribute to all those other unknown and unrecognized Helen Doyles in the Pro-Life movement, who have given of their time, energy, money and reputation, that the defenseless, pre-born citizens of our country may have, as *we* have had, a chance at "life, liberty and the pursuit of happiness" in this world—and eternity with God in the next.

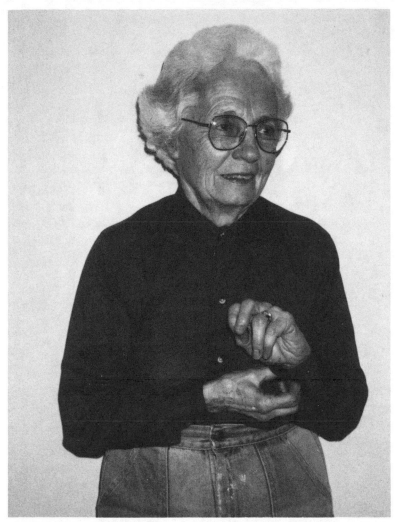

Helen Doyle, veteran Pro-Lifer, who for 6 years has been present at the Rockford abortuary almost every day it is open—in order to pray, protest, and attempt some last-minute crisis counseling. Helen's steadfastness is typical of the courage and perseverance of many "ordinary" and unsung heroes of the Pro-Life movement.

Helen Doyle (left) and Marian Ott, two very faithful Pro-Lifers, at the Rockford abortuary, where Dr. Richard Ragsdale kills children. Altogether, at various locations, Dr. Ragsdale has exterminated 60,000 infants. The Bingo sign advertises that "business as usual" continues in the same building where an estimated 40-50 executions are carried out every week.

NOTES AND SOURCES BY CHAPTERS

1. JOAN (ANDREWS) BELL

1. Joan Andrews and John Cavanaugh-O'Keefe, *I Will Never Forget You* (San Francisco: Ignatius Press, 1989), p. 27.
2. *Ibid.*, p. 75.
3. *Ibid.*, p. 190.
4. Author's notes from Joan Andrews' brief talk at St. John Vianney parish, Chicago area, October 1990.
5. *Ibid.*
6. *Ibid.*
7. *Ibid.*
8. *Ibid.*
9. *Ibid.*
10. *Ibid.*
11. Richard Cowden Guido, ed. *You Reject Them, You Reject Me: The Prison Letters of Joan Andrews.* (Manasses, VA: Trinity Communications, 1988; republished at Brentwood, TN: Wolgemuth & Hyatt, 1989).
12. *Ibid.*

SOURCES FOR CHAPTER—See above.

2. JULIE MAKIMAA

SOURCES FOR CHAPTER:
Ezell, Lee. "Triumph of Love." *Star,* June 2, 1987, p. 25.
Various brochures and pamphlets from Julie Makimaa.

3. GIANNA JESSEN
SOURCES FOR CHAPTER:
Author's meeting with Gianna Jessen, Nov. 10, 1991, Rockford, IL.
Hizer, Gloria. "Gianna Jessen Keeps Her Guardian Angels Busy." *Our Sunday Visitor*, May 31, 1992.
"Local Teens Are Impressed by Abortion 'Miracle-Girl Visitor.'" *Rockford Labor News*, Nov. 15, 1991, p. 4.

4. CAROL EVERETT
1. Carol Everett with Jack Shaw, *The Scarlet Lady: Confessions of a Successful Abortionist* (Brentwood, Tenn.: Wolgemuth & Hyatt, 1991, p. 211.
2. "The Scarlet Lady," *Peter Waldron Live* (tape of radio broadcast), WFEN, Rockford, Illinois, March 10, 1992.
3. *Ibid.*
4. *Ibid.*
5. *Ibid.*
6. *The Scarlet Lady* (book), p. 159.

SOURCES FOR CHAPTER—See above, plus:
Everett, Carol. Presentation in Rockford, IL, January 15, 1989. (Author's notes.)
"Sometimes the Patient Isn't Pregnant at All." *Rockford Labor News*, January 20, 1989, pp. 1,10.
"Tell the Truth," *Rally for Life* video. Anaheim: American Portrait Films International, 1990.

5. CINDI GUASTO
SOURCES FOR CHAPTER:
Biographical information provided by Cindi and Frank Guasto.
Speckhard, Ann. *Psycho-Social Stress Following Abortion*. Kansas City, Missouri: Sheed and Ward, 1987.

6. SHERIFF JAMES HICKEY
SOURCES FOR CHAPTER:
Biographical resume.
Gracia, Guillermo X. "Putting Beliefs Above the Law." *Austin American Statesman*, February 2, 1990, p. A1.
Horvit, Mark. "Graphic Photos Fan Abortion Dispute." *Corpus Christi Caller Times*, January 16, 1990, p. A12.

Horvit, Mark and Mies, John. "Sheriff: My First Duty Is to God." *Corpus Christi Caller Times,* January 20, 1990, p. A10.

7. JAMES DOBSON

1. Jim Manney, "James Dobson: The World's Best-Known Psychologist Is Focused on the Family," *New Covenant,* September 1990, p. 13.
2. "James Dobson, Ph.D. Biographical Information," *Focus On The Family.* (Pamphlet).
3. Rolf Zettersten, *Turning Hearts Toward Home* (Irving, Texas: Word, Inc.), pp. 137-138.
4. *Ibid.,* p. 161.
5. Author's notes from Rally for Life.
6. *Ibid.*
7. *Ibid.*
8. *Ibid.*
9. *Ibid.*
10. James Dobson, "Pro-Life Search for Justice," *Focus On The Family* (Radio Broadcast), June 14, 1990.
11. *Ibid.*
12. *Ibid.*
13. *Ibid.*
14. James Dobson, "Focus Employees Stand for Life," *Focus On The Family* (Radio Broadcast), July 26-27, 1990.
15. James Dobson, "An Abortionist Turns Pro-Life," *Focus On The Family* (Radio Broadcast), December 13-14, 1990.
16. James Dobson, "Children of Rape," *Focus On The Family* (Radio Broadcast), April 4-6, 1990.
17. Biographical information.
18. *Ibid.*

SOURCES FOR CHAPTER—See above, plus:
"Rockford Listeners Hear Pro-Life Win Prediction." *Rockford Labor News,* May 11, 1990, pp. 1,16.

8. FR. PAUL MARX

1. Life after *Casey*—Where We Go from Here" (An Interview with Fr. Paul Marx, O.S.B., Ph.D.), *HLI Reports,* August 1992, p. 3.
2. Michael Engler, "HLI's Purpose, Successes, Problems and Plans" (Engler's interview of Fr. Marx), Human Life International, p. 1.
3. *Ibid.*
4. "Life after *Casey,*" p. 2.
5. *Ibid.,* p. 3.

6. *Ibid.*, p. 2.
7. *Ibid.*, p. 3.
8. *Ibid.*, p. 2.
9. Engler & Marx, p. 2.
10. Fr. Paul Marx, O.S.B., "World-Wide Struggle for Life: at HLI," *HLI Reports*, April/May 1992, p. 3.
11. Rev. Heribert Jone, O.F.M. Cap., J.C.D., ed. by Rev. Urban Adelman, O.F.M. Cap., J.C.D., *Moral Theology* (Westminster, MD: The Newman Press, 1962), p. 542.
12. Marx & Engler, p. 2.
13. *Ibid.*
14. "World-Wide Struggle for Life: at HLI," p. 3.

SOURCES FOR CHAPTER—See above, plus:
    "Meet Father Paul Marx: America's Pro-Life Missionary." *Human Life International* (undated publication), p. 4.

9. BRIAN AND LYNN WOZNICKI

SOURCES FOR CHAPTER:
Biographical information provided by Brian and Lynn.

10. CARDINAL JOHN J. O'CONNOR

1. Fr. Paul Marx, *Confessions of a Pro-Life Missionary* (Gaithersburg, MD: Human Life International, 1988), pp. 75-76.
2. Cardinal John J. O'Connor, "The Choice Is Life: A Respect Life Month Essay by Cardinal O'Connor," *The Catholic Post*, October 28, 1990, p. 10.
3. *Ibid.*
4. *Ibid.*

SOURCES FOR CHAPTER—See above, plus:
    Rally For Life. (Author's notes.)
    "Rockford Joins Thousands in Washington Opposing Slaughter of Unborn Babies." *Rockford Labor News*, May 4, 1990, p. 11.
    Unity 90. (Author's notes.)
    "Unity 90 Participants Urged to Close Ranks for Pro-Life Movement Success." *Rockford Labor News*, July 27, 1990, p. 11.

11. RANDALL TERRY

1. Randall Terry, *Operation Rescue* (Springdale, Pennsylvania: Whitaker House, 1988), cover.

2. *Operation Rescue* by Randall Terry, copyright 1988. Used by permission of the publisher, Whitaker House, Pittsburgh and Colfax Streets, Springdale, Pennsylvania 15144.

3. Randall Terry, *vita*.

4. Randall Terry, *Accessory to Murder* (Brentwood, Tennessee: Wolgemuth & Hyatt, Publishers, Inc., 1990), pp. 158-163.

5. *Ibid.*, pp. 144-146.

6. *Ibid.*, p. 151.

7. *Ibid.*, p. 163.

8. Terry, *vita*.

9. *Ibid.*

10. "Focus on the Family Program Guests Fearful of Speech/Religion Ban," *Rockford Labor News*, July 13, 1990, p. 1.

11. Author's notes from October 1990 rally in Milwaukee, WI.

12. Terry, *Accessory to Murder,* p. 38. Author cites Planned Parenthood Federation of America, *A Five-Year Plan: 1976-1980.*

13. Terry, *Accessory to Murder,* p. 38.

14. Terry, *vita.*

15. Randall Terry, "New Legal Tactic to Turn Tables on Pro-aborts and Brutal Police Who Deny Demonstrators' Right to Lawful Protest!" Advertisement in *The Wanderer*, July 9, 1992, p. 10.

16. Op. cit., Rally.

SOURCES FOR CHAPTER—See above, plus:
　　"Abortion Rescue Leaders in Area." *Rockford Labor News,* November 9, 1990, pp. 1,11.

12. WOODY JENKINS

1. Louis "Woody" Jenkins, "Louisiana's Stand for Life," transcript from speech at Legislators' Educational Conference (sponsored by Americans United For Life), August 20-21, 1990, p. 2.

2. *Ibid.*

3. *Ibid.*, p. 3.

4. *Ibid.*, p. 3.

5. Additional statement by Mr. Jenkins for author.

6. Jenkins, "Louisiana's Stand for Life" (transcript modified by Rep. Jenkins), p. 3.

7. Jenkins, "Louisiana's Stand for Life," p. 4.

8. *Ibid.*, p. 5.

9. *Ibid.*

10. *Ibid.*, p. 6.

11. *Ibid.*

12. *Ibid.*, p. 7.
13. *Ibid.*

SOURCES FOR CHAPTER—See above, plus:
   Andrusko, Dave. "Battle Being Joined in Fight Over Louisiana Abortion Law." *National Right to Life News,* July 30, 1990, p. 18.

13. DON BRADY

1. "A Broadway Butchery? No!" *Rockford Labor News,* November 8, 1985, p. 1.
2. "East Side Awaits First Execution of Unborn Babies," *Rockford Labor News,* December 6, 1985, p. 1.
3. "Profit in Abortion? You Figure It Out," *Rockford Labor News,* November 22, 1985, p. 1.
4. "Where Women May Order the Extermination of Unborn," *Rockford Labor News,* March 16, 1973, p. 1.

SOURCES FOR CHAPTER—See above, plus:
   Author's personal acquaintaince with Don Brady.

14. DOCTOR JOHN C. WILLKE

1. Letter to the author, January 3, 1991.

SOURCES FOR CHAPTER—See above, plus:
   Rally for Life, Washington, D.C., April 28, 1990. (Author's notes.)
   J.C. Willke, Dr. & Mrs. *Handbook on Abortion* (Revised ed.). Cincinnati: Hayes Publishing Co., Inc., 1975.
   Vita: John C. Willke, M.D., January, 1991.

15. JOE SCHEIDLER

1. David Finkel, "Anti-abortionists On Cruise Control," *St. Petersburg Times,* January 13, 1985, Section A, p. 12.
2. *Ibid.*
3. Joe Scheidler, "What We're All About," Pro-Life Action League brochure.
4. *Ibid.*
5. *Ibid.*
6. *Ibid.*
7. *Ibid.*
8. *Ibid.*

9. Statement to the author from Joe Scheidler.

SOURCES FOR CHAPTER—See above, plus:
"Growing Opposition Seen to Slaughter of Unborn as Throngs Take Action: Second Massive Turnout in a Month." *Rockford Labor News,* October 14, 1988, pp. 1,7.
Scheidler, Joe. Presentation in Rockford, IL, October 1988. (Author's notes.)

16. MARY CUNNINGHAM AGEE

1. Mary Cunningham Agee, *Testimony Before Senate Committee on Labor and Human Resources,* May 23, 1990, pp. 1-2.

SOURCES FOR CHAPTER—See above, plus:
Agee, Mary Cunningham. "Answers to Specific Questions." *The Nurturing Network* (undated agency document).
_____. Resume.
_____. Testimony before Senate Committee on Labor and Human Resources. May 23, 1990, pp. 1,2,3,5,7,8.
Bastian, Claire M. "The Nurturing Network: Caring Professionals Network Assistance for Women in Crisis Pregnancies." *The Church World,* June 28, 1990, p. 14.
Tim W. Ferguson. "A Working Woman's Network Into Motherhood." *The Wall Street Journal,* September 4, 1990.
Finley, Mitch. "Mary Cunningham Agee's Nurturing Network: Former Bendix Executive's Alternative to Abortion." *Columbia* Magazine, January, 1991.
Gallagher, John P. "Backstage at TV Debate: Quiet Words Had Impact in the Un-Civil Abortion War." *Catholic New York,* November 29, 1990, p. 13.
Rebeck, Theresa. "Mary Cunningham's Nurturing Network." Reprint from *St. Anthony Messenger,* May, 1989.

17. CYRUS ZAL

1. Paul de Parrie, "The Accused Can Now Have His Say," *The Advocate,* October 1990, p. 19.
2. Doug Hoagland, "Feisty Anti-Abortion Attorney Driven by Faith," *The Fresno Bee,* February 18, 1990, Section G. p. 6.
3. de Parrie, op. cit., p. 18.
4. *Ibid.*
5. *Ibid.*, pp. 18-19.
6. *Ibid.*, p. 18.

7. Heidi H. Holmblad, "Anti-abortion Lawyer Starts Jail Term for Contempt," *The Sacramento Union,* August 10, 1990, Section A, p. 1.
8. Paul de Parrie, "Militant Pro-Life Attorney Finds Himself on the Cutting Edge," *The Advocate,* April 1990, p. 2.
9. *Ibid.*
10. *Ibid.*
11. *Ibid.*
12. de Parrie, "Militant Pro-Life Attorney Finds Himself on the Cutting Edge," p. 2.
13. *Ibid.*

SOURCES FOR CHAPTER—See above.

18. MOTHER TERESA

1. Mother Teresa, *Heart of Joy: The Transforming Power of Self-Giving* (Ann Arbor, MI: Servant, 1987), pp. 65-66.
2. Letter from Mother Teresa to State's Attorney, August 29, 1990.

SOURCES FOR CHAPTER—See above, plus:
   Colson, Charles. *Kingdoms in Conflict.* William Morrow/ Zondervan Publishing House, 1987.
   Petrie, Anne and Jeanette. *Mother Teresa Video.* Burlingame: Red Rose Gallarie, 1986.
   "States Gain more Control as 1 Vote Upholds Roe." *Rockford Register Star,* Tues., June 30, 1992, p. A1.

19. JUDIE BROWN

1. Judie Brown, "Memories and Meditations," *All About Issues,* March 1989, p. 22.
2. *Ibid.*
3. Judie Brown, "What America Life League Does for You," *American Life League: Joining the Winning Team,* 1988, p. 11.
4. Written statement by Judie Brown.
5. Judie Brown, "Don't Miss: Unity 90," *All About Issues,* June-July 1990, p. 27.
6. Judie Brown, "Celebration of Unity: The Unity 90 Experience," *All About Issues,* August/September 1990, p. 26.
7. Judie Brown, "Memories and Meditations," *All About Issues,* p. 23.

SOURCES FOR CHAPTER—See above, plus:
   Vita: Mrs. Brown, President: American Life League.

20. CONGRESSMAN HENRY HYDE

1. "Court Ruling Shifts Abortion Politics," *Congressional Quarterly, Inc.*, Vol. XLV (1989), p. 229.
2. Henry Hyde, speech at 1977 MD Right to Life Convention. (Reprint distributed by Rep. Hyde's office.)

SOURCES FOR CHAPTER—See above, plus:
Colson, Charles. *Kingdoms in Conflict.* William Morrow/Zondervan Publishing House, 1987.
Terry, Randall. *Accessory to Murder.* Brentwood, Tenn: Wolgemuth & Hyatt, Publishers, Inc., 1990.
Written statement by Congressman Hyde.

21. BISHOP AUSTIN VAUGHAN

1. Austin Vaughan, Auxiliary Bishop, New York, "Break the Pro-Abortion Monopoly on Campus!" *The Wanderer,* September 17, 1992, p. 12 (Human Life Alliance advertisement).

SOURCES FOR CHAPTER—See above, plus:
Bishop Vaughan's 1989 Rockford visit. (Author's notes.)
"New York Bishop Makes Impact on Rockford Abortion Debate." *Rockford Labor News,* October 6, 1989, pp. 1-2.

22. PASTOR MATT TREWHELLA

1. Undated brochure from Missionaries to the Preborn.
2. Verbal statement by Msgr. Emmenegger to the author on May 15, 1992.
3. "Missionary Update." Undated newsletter of Missionaries to the Preborn (approx. Sept. 1992).
4. *Ibid.*
5. *Ibid.*
6. *Ibid.*

SOURCES FOR CHAPTER—See above, plus:
Kranz, Cindy. "Operation Rescue Takes Abortion Fight to the Streets." *Rockford Register Star,* November 8, 1991, p. 1-D.
"Man Blockades Milwaukee Abortuary to Protect His Own Child." Bulletin from Missionaries to the Preborn.
"Pastor Matt Trewhella Stirs Rockford Listeners: Churches Should Do More." *Rockford Labor News,* November 22, 1991, p. 11.
Trewhella, Reverend Matthew. "The Protest of a Protestant Minister against Birth Control." *Life Advocate,* July 1992, pp. 10-11.

Video on The Tollway Rescue by Missionaries to the Preborn.
Written statement by Pastor Matt.

23. JAMIE TELLIER

SOURCES FOR CHAPTER:
"Junior High Girl Under Fire: Gave Out Abortion Info." *Rockford Labor News,* May 8, 1992, pp. 1,7.
Likoudis, Paul. "School Seeks Federal Injunction to Prevent Pro-Life Student from Distributing Material." *The Wanderer,* May 7, 1992, p. 8.

24. MONICA MIGLIORINO MILLER

1. Monica Migliorino, "The Burial of the Aborted Unborn," *Homiletic and Pastoral Review,* August-September 1989, pp. 11-18.
2. Written statement sent to the author by Monica Miller.

SOURCES FOR CHAPTER—See above, plus:
Biographical information on Monica Migliorino Miller.

25. CONRAD WOJNAR

1. Conrad Wojnar, "How Much Does It Cost to Save a Baby?" *Vigil Newsletter,* September 1992, p. 2.
2. _____. "When You Pay Your Phone Bill, Think of Us." *Vigil Newsletter,* July 1992, p. 2.
3. _____. "U.S. Supreme Court Stabs Pro-Lifers in the Back." *Vigil Newsletter,* August 1992, p. 2.
4. "How Much Does It Cost to Save a Baby?" p. 2.
5. *Continuing a Decade of Hope for the Unborn.* Banquet program book and report, 1991, of Des Plaines Pro Life Pregnancy Problem Centers, p. 3.

SOURCES FOR CHAPTER—See above, plus:
Wojnar, Conrad. "How Devotion to Mary Led Me to Found Des Plaines Pro Life." *Vigil Newsletter,* November-December 1991.
_____. "N.O.W. and Molly Yard Keep Vicious Lawsuit Alive." *Vigil Newsletter,* November-December 1991, p. 1.
Vigil Newsletter, various issues.

26. GOVERNOR ROBERT CASEY

1. Governor Robert P. Casey, "Remarks of Governor Robert P. Casey,"

National Press Club (transcript), January 27, 1992, p. 1.
2. Governor Robert P. Casey, "Statement to the Democratic National Hearing Committee National Platform Hearing" (transcript), Cleveland, Ohio, May 18, 1992, p. 2.
3. *Ibid.*
4. *Ibid.*
5. Joint opinion quoted by Charles E. Rice, "Casey Ruling Shows the Uselessness of Present Pro-Life Strategy," *The Wanderer*, July 16, 1992.
6. "HB 668," *Laws Of Pennsylvania* (official advance copy), Session of 1988, p. 263.

SOURCES FOR CHAPTER—See above, plus:
Casey, Governor Robert P. *Biographical resumes.*
_____. "The Democratic Party and the Politics of Abortion." Presentation at Notre Dame Law School (transcript), April 2, 1992.
Author's telephone conversation with Richard Spiegelman of Gov. Casey's Office of General Counsel, June 15, 1992.

27. SHARI RICHARD

1. Shari Richard, *Legislative Testimony* (House), March 15, 1990.
2. _____. *Legislative Testimony* (Senate), March 27, 1990.
3. "Warns of Negative Psychological Impact of Sonography in Abortion," *OB/GYN News*, February 15-28, 1986, p. 42.
4. Cf. *American Journal of Obstetrics & Gynecology*, January 1974.

SOURCES FOR CHAPTER—See above, plus:
_____. "Shari Richard's Personal Story" (undated brochure). West Bloomfield, Michigan: Sound Wave Images.
_____. *Ultrasound: A Window to the Womb* video. West Bloomfield, Michigan: Sound Wave Images, 1990.
Schutz, Leslie Hannah. "Unborn Life: Seeing Is Believing." *Pittsburgh Post-Gazette*, June 8, 1990.
"We Need Ultrasound." *Point of View* Radio Talk Show Interview of Shari Richard by Marlin Maddoux, Dallas, TX, March 17, 1992.

28. HELEN DOYLE

SOURCE FOR CHAPTER:
Author's personal acquaintance with Mrs. Doyle.

PRO-LIFE ORGANIZATIONS MENTIONED IN THIS BOOK

American Anti-Persecution
  League (AAPL)
504 S. Beach Blvd., Suite 426
Anaheim, CA 92804

American Life League
P.O. Box 1350
Stafford, VA 22554
(703) 659-4171
Mrs. Judie Brown, President

Citizens for Life
1974 S. 21st St.
Milwaukee, WI 53204
Mrs. Monica M. Miller

Des Plaines Pro Life
4626 N. Knox Ave.
Chicago, IL 60630
(312) 794-1313
Conrad Wojnar, Director

Focus on the Family
P.O. Box 35500
Colorado Springs, CO 80935
(719) 63-FOCUS
Dr. James Dobson, President

Fortress International
P.O. Box 7352
Springfield, IL 62791
(217) 529-9545
Mrs. Julie Makimaa

Human Life Alliance
1840 S. Elena, #103
Redondo Beach, CA 90277
J. T. Finn, President

Human Life International
7845 Airpark Road, Suite E
Gaithersburg, Maryland 20879
(301) 670-7884
Father Paul Marx, O.S.B.,
  President

Life Issues Institute
1802 W. Galbrith Rd.
Cincinnati, OH 45239
(513) 729-3600
Dr. John Willke, President

Life Network
17430 Campbell Road
Dallas, TX 75252
(214) 931-2273
Carol Everett, President

Missionaries to the Preborn
P.O. Box 25204
Milwaukee, WI 53225
(414) 536-1038
Rev. Matt Trewhella

National Right to Life Committee
419 7th St. N.W., Suite 500
Washington, D.C. 20004
(202) 626-8800
Wanda Franz, Ph.D., President

Northern Illinois Crisis Pregnancy
  Center
2501 Broadway
Rockford, IL 61108
(815) 398-5444
Mrs. Pat Palmer, Director

The Nurturing Network
910 Main Street, Suite 360
P.O. Box 2050
Boise, ID 83701
1-800-TNN-4MOM
Mrs. Mary Cunningham Agee,
  Executive Director

Pro-Life Action League
6160 N. Cicero Avenue
Chicago, IL 60646
(312) 777-2900
(312) 777-2525 (24-hour Pro-Life
  News hotline)
Joe Scheidler, Executive Director

Sound Wave Images, Inc.
2422 Harness
West Bloomfield, MI 48324
(313) 360-0743
Shari Richard

ORDER FORM

Quantity Discount

1 copy —7.00		
5 copies—4.00 ea.	$ 20.00 total	
10 copies—3.50 ea.	$ 35.00 total	
15 copies—3.25 ea.	$ 48.75 total	
25 copies—3.00 ea.	$ 75.00 total	
100 copies—2.75 ea.	$ 275.00 total	
500 copies—2.50 ea.	$1,250.00 total	
1,000 copies—2.25 ea.	$2,250.00 total	

Gentlemen:

Please send me _____ copies of **Pro-Life Christians—Heroes for the Pre-born** by Joe Gulotta.

Enclosed is my payment in the amount of _____.

Name _____

Street _____

City _____

State _____ Zip _____

Alternate Payment Plan

Please charge to my _____ VISA _____ MasterCard.

My Account No. is _____

My card expires (give mo. and yr.) _____

Signature _____

All orders mailed promptly. American Customers, please add postage and handling on each order going to one address in the following amounts: For orders of $1-$5, add $1; $5.01-$10, add $2; $10.01-$30, add $3; $30.01-$50, add $4; $50.01-up, add $5. Illinois residents please add 6% sales tax. Canadian residents please add 20% or remit in American currency. Canadian and all other foreign customers please add 20% for surface postage. Foreign customers add 160% for Air Parcel Post, if desired. MasterCard and VISA welcome—send all numbers on your card. For fastest service, telephone or FAX your order—you can have us bill your VISA or MasterCard account. Our FAX number is 815-987-1833. Tel. Toll Free 1-800-437-5876 (Mon.-Fri.—7 a.m.-Midnight; Sat.—8 a.m.-6 p.m., Central Time). Prices guaranteed thru 6/30/94.

TAN BOOKS AND PUBLISHERS, INC.
P.O. Box 424, Rockford, Illinois 61105

Give Copies of This Book...

to friends and relatives, to legislators and doctors, to people in influential positions, but most of all, give copies of this book to young women—to high school and college girls, to those who may be contemplating abortion or may at some time in the future consider it—or who possibly have had an abortion in the past.

Probably no other book brings together so beautifully, so simply and so easily the entire picture of abortion and the Pro-Life effort in our times as *Pro-Life Christians—Heroes for the Pre-born*. Virtually every aspect of abortion is discussed here, and practically the entire case for life is also covered, but all so effortlessly.

Pro-Life Christians is truly one of the most inspiring books of our time—and one of the best, if not *the best* that people today can read on this crucial issue.

Do others a favor by giving copies of this book—that people everywhere will understand the importance of choosing life rather than death in this, the most hotly debated issue of our time. The implications for many will be, literally, a chance to live—as you yourself live who are now reading this page. God will reward you and He will not be outdone in generosity.

For quantity discounts, see the opposite page.

About the Author

Joseph Gulotta is active in a wide range of Pro-Life apostolates from education to Operation Rescue. Believing that the victory for the pre-born will also need to be won on the political front, Mr. Gulotta was a candidate in the primary election for Illinois State Representative.

The author has personally met many of the people profiled in *Pro-Life Christians* at rallies and speeches. In addition, he has communicated with them for this book.

Born in 1948, Joe Gulotta earned a B.S. in Social Studies and an M.S. in Guidance and Counseling from Illinois State University in 1970 and 1971. He studied Theology at the Franciscan University of Steubenville (Ohio) and is a practicing family counselor.

He wrote *Pro-Life Christians* both to encourage those already committed to this cause and to inspire others to become involved—but in addition, to educate those who want to know the truth about one of the most crucial issues of our time.

For speaking engagements, Joe Gulotta may be contacted through Winnebago County Right to Life (326 W. Jefferson St., Rockford, IL 61101) or through the Publisher.

Minnesota Bible College Library
920 Mayowood Rd SW
Rochester, MN 55902